SURVIVING

CULTURE

When Character and Your World Collide

BY EDWARD E. MOODY

randall house

114 Bush Rd | Nashville, TN 37217
randallhouse.com

dedication

To my parents, Ed and Donna Moody,
who taught me how to survive the culture.

table of contents

Introduction

It is a tough time to be a parent. The culture around us is deteriorating. Perhaps you've read or heard the headline, "Brad Pitt and More Stars Go Back on Christian Beliefs."[1] As you look closer you learn that Brad Pitt says he viewed Christianity as stifling, and Katy Perry laments the only book her parents read to her as a child was the Bible. Though they and others like them grew up in Christian environments, they seem to turn away from Christianity. Today, fewer than 18 percent of 18 to 29 year-olds attend church, and the number of atheists and agnostics are on the rise. In fact, one-third of the people under the age of 30 characterize themselves as believing nothing in particular.[2] It is enough to frighten the most confident parent and make one wonder, "How can I prepare my child for this culture?"

I write this book as a parent who has tried to train two children to follow the Lord, as a pastor who has worked with youth and their parents, and a professor who has watched young people for more than 20 years as they've tried to navigate this culture. Rather than being frightened or discouraged, I hope you will see this situation as an opportunity. You need to actively engage the young people in your life rather than being frightened into inaction. Remember the numerous times God has told us to fear not in the Scripture? In fact, as we face this challenge and try to empower our youth let us take Deuteronomy 31:6 to heart, "Be strong and courageous." As we face an increasingly hostile culture, remember what the Lord told Israel as she faced seemingly insurmountable forces, "Do not fear or be in dread of them, for it is the LORD your God who goes with you. He will not leave you nor forsake you." So remember God is not surprised by what is happening in our culture, and He will help you.

Chapter 1

Are They Ready?

In many ways, the culture today is unlike the one you and I experienced as youth. The challenges our youth face is like none before. In other ways, nothing has really changed, as Ecclesiastes 1:9 says, "There is nothing new under the sun."

Some 2,600 years ago, there were parents just like you. They watched as the culture around them deteriorated. They must have feared for their youth. Yet they helped four young men named Daniel, Hananiah, Mishael, and Azariah as they developed into godly adults. These four young men found themselves living in Babylon where there was a god on every corner, and a temple on each block. Yet, instead of succumbing, they held fast. Instead of harming, they were helpful, providing light to those around them. Instead of becoming like the world in which they lived, they pointed those who encountered them to God. Do you want your children to be like that? They can be if you follow the Daniel development plan.

Parents from Another Period

I suspect if you could talk to the parents of Daniel, Hananiah, Mishael, and Azariah, and the others who helped them, they would say to you, "If we could prepare our youth to survive and thrive in Babylon, so can you." How do we know they prepared their children?

How do we know that they were not passive or even lucky parents? After all, we don't really know anything about these parents, or do we? The first significant role any parent has in the life of their child is in the naming of that child. Often after much consternation a child is named. Sometimes it is a family name that is given or the child is named after a friend. But the name matters. Why did these parents name their children Daniel, Hananiah, Mishael, and Azariah?

Names with a Purpose

Judge me, O LORD; for I have walked in mine integrity: I have trusted also in the LORD; therefore I shall not slide.
Psalm 26:1 KJV

Along with knowing the God they worshiped and how He crafted and designed their identity, these Hebrew men carried names with purpose. Daniel means "God is my judge." Did Daniel's parents have Psalm 26 in mind when they named him? When he heard his name, Daniel was reminded that God was watching over him no matter how unjust the world may have seemed. Realizing God is my judge would help him stay on track as he endured various temptations throughout his life. Perhaps as Daniel's parents viewed the injustice around them they chose the name to remind Daniel that God was just and he needed to walk with integrity.

The LORD is merciful and gracious, slow to anger and abounding in steadfast love.
Psalm 103:8

Hananiah means "God has been gracious." Did Hananiah's parents have Psalm 103 in mind when they named him? When he heard his name, Hananiah was reminded that God was good to him regardless of the circumstances he endured. Realizing God is gracious would help him stay on track as he endured difficult times.

> *Who is like the LORD our God,*
> *who is seated on high.*
> *Psalm 113:5*

Mishael means "Who is what God is?" Did Mishael's parents have Psalm 113 in mind when they named him? Perhaps as they viewed the people of Judah worshiping other God's and offering children as sacrifices to Molech they chose the name. When he heard his name, Mishael was reminded of the power of God as he faced a polytheistic environment. When there was a god on every corner (or at every gate around the city), realizing there was no god like Jehovah helped Mishael stay on track.

> *Behold, God is my helper;*
> *the Lord is the upholder of my life.*
> *Psalm 54:4*

Azariah means "God is my help." Did Azariah's parents have Psalm 54 in mind when they named him? When he heard his name, Azariah was reminded of the help that can come only from God as he encountered numerous crises. Realizing God would help him allowed him to endure unimaginable stress and trials.

The naming of these four implies they received strong spiritual preparation in their younger days. Later you will see this was the first place the Chaldeans attacked them.

The names of these four indicate they belonged to Jehovah, the God of Judah just as our children who place their faith in Christ do. Ephesians 4:30 tells us "And do not grieve the Holy Spirit of God, by whom you were sealed for the day of redemption." Christian youth belong to God, but that doesn't mean the culture will not try to change them just as they tried to change Daniel, Hananiah, Mishael, and Azariah by changing their names. The Christian youth are God's, and everything that comes with it. No culture, no pressure, no scientific data, can alter that distinction. With that basis, confidence, hope, and faith, they can grow strong.

Model, Teach, Create

Fortunately, the development of Daniel, Hananiah, Mishael, and Azariah went well beyond the names they were given. Since the days of Moses, faithful Jews have practiced the Shema which is found in Deuteronomy 6:4, "Hear, O Israel: The LORD our God, The LORD is one." I suspect the parents and many of the adults in the lives of Daniel, Hananiah, Mishael, and Azariah recited the Shema as they arose in the morning and just before bedtime. I believe they also served as a model of this passage. Deuteronomy 6:5 says, "You shall love the LORD your God with all your heart and with all your soul and with all your might." As the rest of Judah seemed to chase after other gods, these people followed the one true God. This was a model for the young men that helped them until the end of their lives.

The parents also diligently taught their children as Deuteronomy 6:6-7 instructed, "And these words that I command you today shall be on your heart. You shall teach them diligently to your children, and shall talk of them when you sit in your house, and when you walk by the way, and when you lie down, and when you rise." I believe these parents faithfully taught the Scriptures to these four young men.

Finally, they created an environment where God was honored, and excellence was celebrated. Deuteronomy 6:8-9 says, "You shall bind them as a sign on your hand, and they shall be as frontlets between your eyes. You shall write them on the doorposts of your house and on your gates." Everyone that looked in the home of these four, would find what pointed them to God and encouraged them to serve Him.

What would the parents and youth leaders of Daniel, Hananiah, Mishael, and Azariah say to you? I think they would say, get busy preparing your children for a corrupt culture. In a moment you could be taken away from them. That is what happened to these parents from Judah. In 605 B.C., terror descended upon Judah as an invading army poured into Jerusalem. The economy collapsed, the government was disbanded, and entire neighborhoods disappeared. These four young men found themselves in the middle of horrific events. They were seized and taken to Babylon. (Check out 2 Kings 24 for the entire tale.)

The events these four endured were worse than the Great Depression, the attack upon Pearl Harbor, and the September 11, 2001 attacks combined. After all of this, these youth found themselves in the middle of a corrupt culture being bombarded with its messages. Nothing like this could happen to you, right? Recently, one of my graduate students succumbed after a four-year battle with cancer. He was just 34 years old. He had a wife and four children. His biggest concern was had he prepared his children for the future. He knew he had a limited amount of time before he would be separated from them. Who knows how much time we have with the young people in our lives. Let us use it wisely. Let's study their story to see what we can glean so we can prepare our children to stand.

Identity Development

A major function you have as a parent is the development of identity for your children. Devote a significant effort to identity development knowing that your greatest opportunity to influence them is early in life.

The Bible says in Ephesians 6:10-11, 13, "Finally, be strong in the Lord and in the strength of his might. Put on the whole armor of God, that you may be able to stand against the schemes of the devil.

Therefore take up the whole armor of God, that you may be able to withstand in the evil day, and having done all, to stand firm." I believe Daniel, Hananiah, Mishael, and Azariah knew the Lord and put on the whole armor of God before they were taken from Judah. To survive and thrive in their culture, our children also need to place their faith in the Lord and derive their strength from Him by putting on the whole armor of God.

Young people will fail if they are not prepared. Entering the corrupt culture unprepared is akin to a well-meaning firefighter entering a burning building without the proper equipment. A lack of preparation sets your children up to become a victim of the corrupt culture. Preparation begins with instilling a sense of certainty.

If Daniel, Hananiah, Mishael, and Azariah had not been certain about who they were, their lives would have been very different. When their world turned upside down they were stable enough to stand upright. Who are you when you are Judean, and Judah lies in ruins? Who are you when you are a Christian and the culture cheapens Christ? What are you to do when the kingdom you've spent your life preparing to serve has been conquered? How do you react when the culture attacks what is important to you?

Daniel, Hananiah, Mishael, and Azariah's situation would be like dreaming of working in the United States government, only to see the nation collapse and find yourself working in the capitol of the invading country. Daniel, Hananiah, Mishael, and Azariah found themselves serving in the kingdom that destroyed their homeland, and perhaps killed many they loved. When they entered Babylon they found themselves in a land that was unlike anything they had seen. The Babylonians were experts in magic devoted to other gods. Daniel and his friends were immersed into this culture. They found themselves in classrooms studying polytheistic literature where magic, sorcery, charms, and astrology were valued. Yet, they were unlike many of the young people who accompanied them and began taking on the ways of Babylon. Perhaps many of their peers left behind their "outdated and obsolete" faith as they entered the largest city the world had known to that point in history.

Yet, these young men were secure enough in their relationship with God and their knowledge of God to be able to study this material without it undermining their faith. Their previous time with God and study of Scripture had prepared them to withstand this onslaught of false teaching. They knew God, therefore, they were undeterred. Similarly, our children may find themselves bombarded with evolution, polytheism, and moral relativism where wrong is portrayed as right and right as wrong; so they too must be certain of their identity, relationship with God, and what they believe.

A Challenge Emerges

Babylon in the Bible

> . . . And he brought them to <u>the land of Shinar</u>, to the house of his god, and placed the vessels in the treasury of his god.
> Daniel 1:2

The land of Shinar is where the tower of Babel was built.

> And as people migrated from the east, they found a plain in <u>the land of Shinar</u> and settled there.
> Genesis 11:2

Shinar and Babylon are used in the Bible to describe corruption and immorality. Consider the reference to Babylon in the book of Revelation.

> And on her forehead was written a name of mystery: "<u>Babylon</u> the great, mother of prostitutes and of earth's abominations."
> Revelation 17:5

Babylon is anywhere you find a crooked and perverse culture.

As our children enter the culture, the forces of that culture will try to change them. In the Bible, Babylon always refers to a place of corruption. Interestingly, Daniel writes they were taken to the land of Shinar (Daniel 1:2), where there was an immediate assault upon their identity. That came in the form of a name change.

Daniel's name was changed to Belteshazzar that meant, "May a god protect his life" or "A goddess protect the king." Hananiah's name was changed to Shadrach that may invoke the name of the Babylonian god Marduk. Mishael's name was changed to Meshach and the meaning of this name is less certain. Azariah's name was changed to Abednego, which may mean "Servant of (the god) Nabu."[3] The king was probably immersing the youth in the customs of the Chaldeans so that Judah might become a distant memory. Similarly, our youth will be attacked when they enter their Babylon. Perhaps it will be an assault on their identity like, "Jesus was just a man," and "The Bible is just a manmade book." They may even see their faith described as something they do not recognize. Daniel, Hananiah, Mishael, and Azariah were undeterred when the Babylonians changed their names. We too want our youth to be undeterred by attacks on their faith. For this to occur they must be immersed in the Word of God and have a deep relationship with God.

The Bible, Their Best Friend

Stand therefore, <u>having fastened on the belt of truth,</u> and having put on the breastplate of righteousness, and, as shoes for your feet, having put on the readiness given by the gospel of peace.
Ephesians 6:14-15

Daniel and his friends didn't become scholars of the Torah overnight. They most likely studied it from childhood. How was this accomplished? Deuteronomy 6:7 says, "You shall teach them diligently to your children, and shall talk of them when you sit in your house, and when you walk by the way, and when you lie down, and when you rise." This means that we must talk a lot about what the Scripture says and actively teach it to the youth in our lives.

When a person becomes a follower of Christ, the Holy Spirit doesn't magically endow them with the ability to write a commentary on Revelation. God didn't design spiritual growth that way.

Children do not grow physically without a steady diet. The tendency is to eat at least three times a day. When they miss a meal they aren't up to their peak performance level. In addition, eating a balanced diet is important. Though our children might think a diet of chips and soda would be wonderful, we know eventually it will have a negative impact upon them. If there is anything missing from a person's diet, they don't operate at their optimal level physically and are more susceptible to disease.

Just like muscles or healthy bones are not developed by a hit and miss diet or a binge on veggies, spiritual growth is derived from a steady diet in the Bible. Our children can grow in the Word through small group study, Sunday School classes, Christian Education

> **Helpful Resources:**
>
> Bible
> Notebook for recording
> Unger's Bible Handbook
> M. E. Unger, & G. Larson (2005). *The New Unger's Bible Handbook.* Chicago, IL: Moody Publishers.

courses, and listening to sermons. But encourage them to have a time of personal Bible reading as Deuteronomy 17:19 teaches us, "And it shall be with him, and he shall read in it all the days of his life, that he may learn to fear the Lord his God by keeping all the words of this law and these statutes, and doing them."

To benefit from the Bible, encourage them to gather the tools they will need just as one gathers utensils before a meal. Get them a readable Bible in a translation they understand, a Bible dictionary or handbook that will help them get some context for what they are reading. Also get a journal or notebook for them to record what they are learning and what they need to apply to their life. This allows them to process the Word just as the body processes food.

Encourage them to ask God to direct them as they study the Bible and to help them apply it to their life. I like the ESV study Bible. It is a good idea to compare passages in different translations at the Bible-gateway.com website or with the Biblegateway or YouVersion apps.

It helps to ask key questions about a text as one reads it like:

- What did this passage mean to the original hearers?
- What is the timeless principle?
- What does it teach me about God?
- Based on this passage, how can I apply it?

After answering these questions they can use a journal or note-book to record their observations, what they learn about God, and what they need to apply to their life. Regularly ask your child about what parts of the Scripture they are studying and what they are learn-ing. It helps if they are able to have times and places where they read the Bible and pray so that it becomes a habit in their life.

Why does this matter? People who are in top physical shape are more likely to survive an injury or sudden illness. Their bodies draw upon the strength they have developed when injured. Similarly, when faced with a spiritual crisis they must draw upon the strength they've developed over time and their relationship with the Lord if they are to endure.

Daniel, Hananiah, Mishael, and Azariah knew their God well, long before the Babylonians tried to change their name. Similarly, our teens can't wait to develop a relationship with God until they find themselves in situations when they are the only Christian around and people are trying to change them.

*In all circumstances take up the shield of faith, with
which you can extinguish all the flaming darts of the
evil one; and take the helmet of salvation, and the
sword of the Spirit, which is the word of God.*
Ephesians 6:16-17

Application of the Word

You will see later that the faith of Daniel, Hananiah, Mishael, and Azariah, as well as their application of the Word of God, helped them deal with multiple attacks (or flaming darts of the evil one). Application of the Word of God is to spiritual growth as exercise is to physical growth. Unused biblical knowledge is similar to unused muscles. Without use, deterioration results.

By keeping the Bible before them as instructed in Deuteronomy 6:7-8 our teens can be equipped to deal with various problems. For example, Dr. Dan Ariely conducted some research indicating that cheating is prevalent on college campuses. He found one situation where people were less likely to cheat. One group of students was asked to recall the Ten Commandments before taking a test.[4] Most of these students did not know the Ten Commandments and none could recall all of them. However, taking the time to recall them and consider some of them significantly reduced cheating. This demonstrates that taking the time to think about the Word of God can help them stay on track. Imagine the results that could be achieved for a person motivated to obey the Word.

With each step our youth take applying the Bible to their life, they are strengthening themselves for the challenges they will face in the future. They should also find that their relationship with the Lord grows deeper. Applying the Word leads to the Word abiding in them and an intimate knowledge of it and the Lord. When they face a problem, we want them to ask, "What does the Bible say about this? We can model this by taking the Bible and applying it to the problems that arise. As an example, consider Psalm 46. If Daniel, Hananiah, Mishael, and

Azariah knew this passage, how might they have applied it? How might our youth apply it in their own lives?

The Worst Case Scenario Psalm
Psalm 46

God is our refuge and strength, a very present help in trouble. Therefore we will not fear though the earth gives way, though the mountains be moved into the heart of the sea, though its waters roar and foam, though the mountains tremble at its swelling. Selah (emphasis mine).

What did this passage mean to the original hearers? It meant that God was with them as they were encountering great difficulty and he would help them. The mountains falling into the middle of the sea would be the most traumatic event one could imagine (e.g., like the overthrow of your nation or the death of a parent). Instead of fear, the reader is instructed to concentrate upon God's ability to help them in any situation, even one so desperate as the mountains falling into the sea.

What is the timeless principle? God provides refuge and strength for us at the worst times of our lives.

What do I learn about God? He will be my refuge, my strength in the most difficult moments of my life.

What do I need to do based upon this passage? Ask yourself, "What are the worst events that could transpire in my life?" Think about how God would help you and give you strength during these. God will be with you when your world is turned upside down and when your life is calm. God is our refuge, our help, every day all the time. You don't know what the future holds, but you can know that God will help you, especially at the most difficult time of a crisis.

Encourage youth to have a period daily where they pause and reflect upon God. It is this kind of work that will help them as they encounter various difficulties in their life. As they look at Scripture like this, ask them to consider how the same God who helped Jacob and Daniel, Hananiah, Mishael, and Azariah will help them.

I like reading *The Complete Worst-Case Scenario Survival Handbook*. There is an entry about how to escape from a giant octopus, and a charging rhino. Then there are more serious entries like surviving if your parachute doesn't open, and evading a stampede of shoppers. Some are pretty silly but others are fairly serious like surviving a rollover in a car, or how to perform a tracheotomy.

While we truly have no idea what the future holds for our youth in terms of personal triumphs and tragedies (giant octopi or not) or in terms of the evolution of our culture, God does know. He is preparing them today for what they will face tomorrow.

God knew what would happen to Daniel, Hananiah, Mishael, and Azariah. Isaiah 39:7 says, "And some of your own sons, who will come from you, whom you will father, shall be taken away, and they shall be eunuchs in the palace of the king of Babylon." This verse was written between 750 and 690 B.C., yet Isaiah prophesied about the events of 605 B.C. during Daniel, Hananiah, Mishael, and Azariah's life. God also knows what will happen in the future to our children.

Since our culture so actively attacks the Bible it is important to equip our youth to explain it. Incidentally, the book of Daniel is one of the favorite targets of critics. Many deny that Daniel was a prophet because in Hebrew Bibles Daniel is located in the Writings section. Some claim that someone other than Daniel wrote the book of Daniel, and that Daniel was not written until the second century B.C.

As an example of how to address these issues, consider a brief defense of the book of Daniel. The book of Daniel was likely located in the Writings section of the Hebrew Bible because Daniel's ministry was to the heathen court rather than the people of Israel.

By reading the New Testament one will clearly see that Jesus viewed Daniel as a prophet, and his book as truth. Matthew 24:15 says, "So when you see the abomination of desolation spoken by the prophet Daniel, standing in the holy place (let the reader understand)."

Ezekiel, a contemporary of Daniel wrote highly of him: "Even if these three men, Noah, Daniel, and Job, were in it, they would deliver but their own lives by their righteousness, declares the Lord GOD. Even if Noah, <u>Daniel</u>, and Job were in it, as I live, declares the Lord GOD, they would deliver neither son nor daughter. They would deliver but their own lives by their righteousness (Ezekiel 14:14, 20).

Some have claimed that Ezekiel was referring to a different Daniel but consider Ezekiel 28:3, "You are indeed wiser than Daniel; no secret is hidden from you." Ezekiel's Daniel sounds like the one in the book that bares his name. Sometimes our youth will need to utilize other valuable resources to defend Scripture. For example, in Daniel: Tyndale Old Testament Commentary by J. G. Baldwin, they can learn that the book of Daniel refers to people and events that would not otherwise be known from biblical events or history.[5]

Other commentators indicate there is nothing in the original Hebrew and Aramaic language of the book that precludes an authorship of the sixth century B.C.[6]

When they find they need to learn more about a particular book of the Bible, they can utilize commentaries. Many of these can be found in libraries, however, not all will be helpful. Teach them to look for commentaries by those who believe the Bible is the inspired Word of God. There are two books that rank commentaries according to reliability: Old Testament Commentary Survey by T. Longman and New Testament Commentary Survey by D. A. Carson.

Critics like to attack the biblical account of creation and the historical accuracy of the Bible so it helps to be familiar with work that addresses these attacks. You can inoculate your youth by getting them to read some of the great works on these subjects. Here is a list of resources where you can find podcasts that will help prepare you for these issues.

Podcast Resources
See also survivingculture.com

Title	Description	Website
Answers . . . with Ken Ham	Daily podcast about Creation	www.answersingenesis.org
Apologetics 315 Interviews	315 interviews of Christian apologists	www.apologetics315.com
Coffee Cup Apologetics	Brief enough to have apologetics over lunch	www.ccapologetics.wordpress.com
Defenders Podcast	Dr. William Lane Craig's Sunday School class on Christian doctrine and apologetics	www.reasonablefaith.org
The Voice of Truth	4 minute apologetic updates from Dr. Norman Geisler	www.normangeisler.net
Josh McDowell Ministry	Weekly messages from Josh McDowell	www.joshradio.org
Lee Strobel	Find answers to your faith questions	www.leestrobel.com
Ravi Zacharias International Ministries	Helping the thinkers believe; helping the believers to think	www.rzim.org

In addition, you can find many books that address these questions.

Ken Ham, *The New Answers in Genesis Boxed Set (Vol. 1-3)*—A close look at questions about evolution.

C. S. Lewis, *The C. S. Lewis Signature Classics*—Includes *Mere Christianity, The Screwtape Letters, The Problem of Pain.*

Josh McDowell, *The New Evidence That Demands a Verdict*—Two bestselling volumes in one, a classic defense of the faith.

Josh McDowell and Sean McDowell, *More Than a Carpenter*—Finding real answers in Jesus Christ.

Josh McDowell and Dave Sterrett, *Is the Bible True . . . Really? A Dialogue on Skepticism, Evidence and Truth*—Questions about the truthfulness of the Bible answered from the standpoint of a college freshman in a state university.

Lee Strobel, *The Case for Christ*—A former atheistic journalist examines the history of the Christian faith.

Lee Strobel, *The Case for a Creator*—A former atheistic journalist examines evidence for a Creator.

Lee Strobel, *The Case for Faith*—A former atheistic journalist examines some of the tough questions often asked of the Christian faith.

Ravi Zacharias, *Beyond Opinion: Living the Faith We Defend*—How to defend your faith and be transformed by it.

Ravi Zacharias, *Jesus Among Other Gods*—Examines the unique truth of the Christian message and exposes the futility of other religions.

It is important to remember that not every accusation or sin or heresy needs to be addressed by our youth. However, they can expect at one time or another—and likely many times—in their lives, they will need to provide a defense of what they believe, what God teaches about Himself and His relationship to the world.

Instead of dodging questions about evolution and so forth we want them to be confident and competent enough to look for opportunities to address these issues. By the way, teach them when they get those opportunities to be clear, concise, and congenial. Also, they should consider whether they are dealing with a seeker or a scoffer.

A Diet Change

Real Christianity impacts the way we live. Our youth can expect many assaults upon their character just as Daniel and his friends experienced. The Babylonians placed Daniel and his friends in challenging situations. As part of the training program the Babylonians presented the youth with Babylonian food. For many this may not seem like a problem, but there is more going on under the surface. Think about how food is integrally intertwined with culture. Consider the authentic food found in places like Chinatown in cities like San Francisco and New York or barbeque from North Carolina or Kansas City. We tend to talk about food when we speak of going home, and consider traditional dishes "comfort food."

The Babylonian food may have been a kind of gift, and a gift isn't always a gift. Psychologist Robert Cialdini wrote about how people are influenced. He notes that we are likely to comply with requests from others after receiving an unsolicited gift.[7] Perhaps that is what Nebuchadnezzar had in mind by the food he provided here. If they'd eaten this food, they would be more likely to comply with other requests in the future. It is little things, often subtle in nature that are used to assail a persons character so teach your children to be careful what they say yes to.

> Behold, I am sending you out as sheep
> in the midst of wolves, so be wise as serpents
> and innocent as doves.
> Matthew 10:16

The most important grievance against this food is that Scripture forbade it. This proves that these four youth were skilled at applying the Scripture in how they lived their lives. In Leviticus, we learn that a Jew was forbidden to eat certain foods lest he defile himself. "You shall not make yourselves detestable with any swarming thing that swarms, and you shall not <u>defile</u> yourselves with them, and become unclean through them. For I am the LORD your God. <u>Consecrate yourselves</u> therefore, and be holy, for I am holy. You shall not <u>defile</u> yourselves with any swarming thing that crawls on the ground. For I am the LORD who brought you up out of the land of Egypt to be your God. You shall therefore be holy, for I am holy" (Leviticus 11:43-45, emphasis added).

Other dietary restrictions can be found in Deuteronomy and Isaiah. "Depart, depart, go out from there; <u>touch no unclean thing</u>; go out from the midst of her; purify yourselves, you who bear the vessels of the LORD" (Isaiah 52:11, emphasis added). "Only be sure that you do not eat the blood...<u>You shall not eat it</u>, that all may go well with you and with your children after you" (Deuteronomy 12:23-25, emphasis added). Note that eating these foods would lead to a Jew being defiled.

Perhaps the Babylonians required this food as an attack upon the conscience of the Jews. Furthermore, the food may have already been offered to a Babylonian god. Therefore, eating the meat would have been the equivalent of recognizing and honoring the god the food had been offered to. For all practical purposes Daniel, Hananiah, Mishael, and Azariah would have been denying the claims Jehovah had made as the one true God. The meat probably was not prepared in keeping with the food preparation regulations God had provided, which would have also been a method of defiling these Jews.

How did Daniel respond, "But Daniel <u>resolved</u> that he would not <u>defile</u> himself with the king's food, or with the wine that he drank. Therefore he asked the chief of the eunuchs to allow him not to <u>defile</u> himself" (Daniel 1:8, emphasis added). Daniel concluded that accepting this food would compromise his character. He resolved not to defile himself. He demonstrated remarkable wisdom as he discussed this matter with the Babylonian chief who indicated that the consequence for failure in the training program would be death. Daniel 1:10 reads, "And the chief of the eunuchs said to Daniel, 'I fear my lord the king, who assigned your food and your drink; for why should he see that you were in worse condition than the youths who are of your own age? So you would endanger my head with the king.'"

Purity

The attack upon our youth is more likely to come in the form of an attack upon purity. The Bible says in 2 Timothy 2:21, "Therefore, if anyone cleanses himself from what is dishonorable, he will be a vessel for honorable use, set apart as holy, useful to the master of the house, ready for every good work." When Daniel, Hananiah, Mishael, and Azariah arrived in Babylon, they were standing in the largest city the world had seen until that time. They encountered great temptation. The real issue with the Babylonian food was whether these Judean youth would remain pure. The temptation with this food was an attempt to defile their hearts.

Our youth will face similar challenges to compromise their purity. Their challenges will be more along the line of 2 Timothy 2:22, "Flee youthful passions and pursue righteousness, faith, love, and peace, along with those who call on the Lord from a pure heart." Today most youth use alcohol and other drugs and find themselves immersed in the sexual hook-up culture. Should our youth choose to follow the biblical standard on sexual relationships, they will be in the minority. Between 60 percent and 80 percent of American college students have had intimate sexual experiences with people they do not even know.[8]

And he said, "What comes out of a person is what defiles him. For from within, out of the heart of man, come evil thoughts, sexual immorality, theft, murder, adultery, coveting, wickedness, deceit, sensuality, envy, slander, pride, foolishness. All these evil things come from within, and they defile a person."
Mark 7:20-23

In fact, 70 percent of sexually active 12 to 21 year-olds report having had uncommitted sex within the last year.[9] This behavior leads to serious consequences like assaults, sexually transmitted diseases, poor academic performance as well as other problems. In a sample of undergraduate students from Canada, 78 percent of women and 72 percent of men who had uncommitted sex reported a history of experiencing regret after such an encounter.[10] Had Daniel, Hananiah, Mishael, and Azariah ate the food described in Daniel 1, they would have experienced this same regret, which would have impeded their ability to influence others.

Our youth should also expect challenges in the area of alcohol and other drugs. In a major study, 68.9 percent of college students reported drinking alcohol in the previous 30 days.[11] Each year, more than 1,825 college students die from alcohol-related accidents and nearly 600,000 are injured while drunk. Another 696,000 are assaulted by another student who has been drinking, and 97,000 are victims of alcohol-related sexual assault or date rape. Twenty-five percent of college students report academic consequences related to alcohol.[12]

Several studies have indicated that living circumstances can put one at greater risk for these behaviors. Students who reside in a fraternity residence in secular universities are at greatest risk. In fact, there is a seven-fold increase in drinking behavior as compared to students who stay in a dorm or apartment. Also, living in a dormitory instead of living at home with parents is associated with substantially higher levels of alcohol use and alcohol–related adverse consequences.[13] The temptation of sex, alcohol, and other drugs is an attempt to defile their heart and impede their ability to influence others. Should our youth choose to remain pure in these areas they will be following in the steps of Daniel, Hananiah, Mishael, and Azariah. When they make the decision to follow God and stay pure it can help them to keep from defiling themselves, and instead of becoming a victim of the culture, they can be used of God to influence the culture.

Do Hard Things

O LORD, who shall sojourn in your tent?...He who walks blamelessly and does what is right and speaks truth in his heart;...who swears to his own hurt and does not change;...He who does these things shall never be moved.
Psalm 15:1-5

Psalm 15 teaches that those who follow the Lord are willing to do hard things, walk blamelessly, and tells the truth even when it hurts. Difficult actions and choices often reveal a persons character. It can be easy to follow the Lord when a young person faces little resistance. We find out what kind of character a person has once they encounter challenges that demand they do hard things. The resulting decisions determine what the person becomes since we are a product of our decisions. Prepare a young person for the ways their character will be assaulted in the future, and help them prepare to do the hard things to keep themselves pure from defilement. Good decisions tend to lead to more good decisions. Bad decisions tend to lead to more bad decisions. If these four had said yes to Babylon by defiling themselves with this food they would have placed themselves on a different trajectory in life, which would have led to further compromises and more distance from their identity and their God. They concluded that honoring God was more important than life itself.

Help your young person develop godly habits (e.g., daily Bible reading, regular church attendance, fellowship with other believers, helping others). When stressed, people revert to old habits—even good ones. For a semester, researchers collected data on a group of undergraduates' eating, exercise, and other behaviors. When students were sleep-deprived they were more likely to stick to old habits. Students who ate unhealthy pastries or doughnuts for breakfast ate even more during exams. Similarly, people who went to the gym were more likely to go to the gym when stressed.[14] If our young people are in the habit of reading their Bibles, they are more likely to keep reading them in a crisis.

Certain in Resolve

Daniel was told failing to eat the food would endanger his life. Would this information dissuade Daniel from his resolution? No, Daniel and his friends were committed to the God they knew and loved. They remained firm in their resolve not to partake of this food. Fortunately, these youth stayed firm. Daniel suggested they be allowed to eat vegetables rather than defile themselves. That request was honored by the steward that worked with them. They held onto their identity.

One Decision Leads to Another
What might have been

The lives of these four could have turned out very differently. It is unlikely they would have stood their ground at the fiery furnace some twenty years later. Perhaps decades later Daniel would have refused to pray to spare himself from the lion's den.

Chapter 2

Do They Have Substance?

Try to prepare your youth so they will not succumb to the trend toward mediocrity. You may have seen the bumper sticker that says, "Mediocrity takes a lot less time, and most people won't notice the difference." So, what is wrong with mediocrity? A lot!

Consider how we dislike mediocrity in our favorite sports teams. Years ago my family and I watched the New York Yankees play the Texas Rangers. Whatever you think about the Yankees, you know they have a strong dislike for mediocrity. There was an attitude of expectation of a good performance, especially for some of their highly paid superstars.

At one point, New York was down 5-2. Yet, there was this sense that the Yankees could come back. Around the fifth inning, I went to get some snacks. Before I could come back, the Yankees had taken the lead and went on to win the game. Later that year, they won the World Series.

The next year we went to San Francisco to see the Giants play the Los Angeles Dodgers. They lost; in fact, it was the last of a three game sweep by the Dodgers. There was a sense of great displeasure. The next day, in the *San Francisco Chronicle*, we learned that the manage-

As you work with your youth, frequently talk about decisions. Look at history for examples of decisions you can discuss. Also, discuss issues that are in the news about celebrities, politicians, and other media figures as opportunities to discuss the consequences of good and bad decisions. You can even use the films and books they see as discussion opportunities. Frequently ask, "What if?" How might a life have been different, for good or bad if a different decision had been made? The decisions our youth make today will set their life trajectory. If they make good decisions it will become easier for them to continue on that path.

> Then _Arioch brought in Daniel before the king in haste_ and said thus to him: "I have found among the exiles from Judah a man who will make known to the king the interpretation."
> Daniel 2:25

Help Them Know God

Teach your children to pray about everything. If they are worried about a bully, a bad grade, or even their health, pray with them about that. Model prayer in your life, as they hear and observe you pray about various difficulties. Daniel, Hananiah, Mishael, and Azariah consistently prayed.

Nebuchadnezzar had a dream that is recorded in Daniel 2. He became enraged when the wise men of the day could not tell him the meaning of the dream. He was convinced they were trying to deceive him and decided to kill the wise men and their families.

Arioch, the captain of the king's guard, approached Daniel to kill Daniel, Hananiah, Mishael, and Azariah. Daniel calmly asked Arioch for time. Then he asked Hananiah, Mishael, and Azariah to pray.

Daniel Prayed

> *Blessed be the LORD, the God of Israel, from ever-*
> *lasting to everlating! Amen and Amen.*
> *Psalm 41:13*

Daniel began to pray, "<u>Blessed</u> be the name of God <u>forever and ever</u>, to whom belong wisdom and might" (Daniel 2:20, emphasis added). Though Daniel's life was at stake, and he was under great stress, he prayed a prayer similar to Psalm 41:13, as well as a similar prayer offered by Job. This shows us that he turned to his Savior in his most difficult moments and recognized God's ability to take care of him. This was a habit.

He enumerated the reasons why the name of God should be eternally blessed. The prayer distinguishes God from the idols of Babylon.

> *With God are <u>wisdom</u> and might;*
> *he has counsel and <u>understanding</u>.*
> *Job 12:13*

In Daniel 2:21, he prays, "He changes times and seasons; he removes kings and sets up kings; he gives <u>wisdom</u> to the wise and knowledge to those who have <u>understanding</u>" (emphasis added). Note how the prayer reminds us of statements Job made about the Lord. God alone is the author of wisdom. Daniel gives Him credit for his success.

> *He uncovers the <u>deeps</u> out of <u>darkness</u> and brings*
> *deep darkness to light.*
> *Job 12:22*

Daniel prays about the deep and the secret things of God in Daniel 2:22, "He reveals <u>deep</u> and hidden things; he knows what is in the <u>darkness</u>, and the light dwells with him." Again, note the similarities to Job.

Daniel recognized that it was God who could save him and God did. His relationship with God brought him through this difficulty and allowed him to survive and thrive in the midst of the crisis. The scriptural quality of his prayers indicate that he had a deep relationship with the Lord which strengthened him in the crisis.

Source of Strength

The source of this calmness became evident some 20 years later when Hananiah, Mishael, and Azariah refused to bow to an image Nebuchadnezzar had made. Daniel 3:7 tells us, "Therefore, as soon as all the peoples heard the sound of the horn, pipe, lyre, trigon, harp, bagpipe, and every kind of music, <u>all the peoples</u>, nations, and languages fell down and worshiped the golden image that King Nebuchadnezzar had set up."

Psychologist Robert Cialdini writes that peer pressure is more alluring when it seems that everyone is doing something. Even the best of us can begin to feel like everyone is doing something. Here it seemed like everyone was bowing down to the image. That put the pressure upon Hananiah, Mishael, and Azariah to go along. Yet, they did not bow.

Nebuchadnezzar threatened them, and gave them another chance. They remained firm. They said, "O Nebuchadnezzar, <u>we have no need to answer you in this matter</u>. If this be so, our God whom we serve is able to deliver us from the burning fiery furnace, and he will deliver us out of your hand, O king. <u>But if not</u>, be it known to you, O king, that we will not serve your gods or worship the golden image that you have set up" (Daniel 3:16-18, emphasis added).

Basically, they say to the man who has the power to take their lives, "There is nothing to discuss here." Yet, this was not an idle threat. Nebuchadnezzar had killed people in this manner before (Jeremiah 29:22).

However, they responded by saying, "We have a God that can save us; we will not bow down to your god." In other words, "Our God may choose to save us, but if not, we will die remaining faithful to Him." Nebuchadnezzar was trying to come between these four youth and their relationship with God. We want to convey to our youth that God can protect them, "but if not" they should follow Him no matter what. That relationship should be so strong they would rather die than do something that might come between them and God. It is that relationship that allowed them to survive and thrive in Babylon. Our youth too can survive in our culture if they have this kind of relationship with the Lord no matter what the world does to them. You are not alone. Remember, Hebrews 12:1 tells us that we are surrounded by a cloud of witnesses. Who knows, maybe the parents that raised Daniel, Hananiah, Mishael, and Azariah are part of that group. They just might be cheering you on as you raise the children in your life.

Dunkirk—A Twentieth Century Example

In June of 1940 at a low point in World War II, Hitler's armies were about to destroy the British Army that was trapped on the beaches at Dunkirk. The army sent a three-word message to the British people. "And if not." This is the phrase translated "But if not" in this passage where Hananiah, Mishael, and Azariah responded to Nebuchadnezzar. When the British people heard this message from the British Army they immediately recognized the reference to Shadrach, Meshach, and Abednego. They knew the Army was saying, "Our God can deliver us, but if not we will remain faithful and die on those beaches." The British people responded by going out in thousands of boats to save their army.[15] Do we, and our youth, know this passage as well as the British did in 1940? It is critical that young people know Scripture and are able to apply it. You can say that the knowledge and application of this passage saved the British Army at Dunkirk and enabled Britain to survive World War II.

Bring it All Together

Model

The parents of Daniel, Hananiah, Mishael, and Azariah probably served as a model for them by standing against the evil in Judah. You can do similarly by pushing against the status quo in our own culture. Be busy reading and applying your Bible, praying, and being engaged in your church. Show your youth the way.

Teach

It appears from the story thus far that Daniel, Hananiah, Mishael, and Azariah had been taught the instruction found in Leviticus 11 about the foods that would defile them. These foods seemed to repulse them. You can do similarly by teaching your youth biblical teaching about sexual intimacy and substance abuse resulting in them being repulsed by these things as well. Daniel, Hananiah, Mishael, and Azariah had probably been taught passages like Psalm 46. Similarly, you can teach passages like Philippians 4 to youth who are dealing with a difficult test, a bully, or anything that might lead them to be anxious.

Create

I suspect the parents of Daniel, Hananiah, Mishael, and Azariah created an environment where it was clear that God was their number one priority. There were probably many things in their environment to remind them of this. You can create an environment where the tools for Bible study are readily available, and where the church is a major part of the life of the family. Create an environment where the things of God are honored. Talk about Christian actors, actresses, musicians, politicians, scientists, and so forth so that it becomes clear that "everyone isn't doing it."

Do They Have Substance?

Try to prepare your youth so they will not succumb to the trend toward mediocrity. You may have seen the bumper sticker that says, "Mediocrity takes a lot less time, and most people won't notice the difference." So, what is wrong with mediocrity? A lot!

Consider how we dislike mediocrity in our favorite sports teams. Years ago my family and I watched the New York Yankees play the Texas Rangers. Whatever you think about the Yankees, you know they have a strong dislike for mediocrity. There was an attitude of expectation of a good performance, especially for some of their highly paid superstars.

At one point, New York was down 5-2. Yet, there was this sense that the Yankees could come back. Around the fifth inning, I went to get some snacks. Before I could come back, the Yankees had taken the lead and went on to win the game. Later that year, they won the World Series.

The next year we went to San Francisco to see the Giants play the Los Angeles Dodgers. They lost; in fact, it was the last of a three game sweep by the Dodgers. There was a sense of great displeasure. The next day, in the *San Francisco Chronicle*, we learned that the management made some big moves, and their first baseman, Buster Posey, was moved to catcher. Before the changes, they were an okay (mediocre) baseball team. After the changes, they excelled. Later that year, they won the World Series.

Next, we saw the Chicago Cubs at Wrigley Field. They took an early lead only to eventually fall behind. You had a sense they were going to lose, that the lead was insurmountable. I went to get some snacks; and when I returned, they were even further behind. They lost. They didn't even make the wildcard playoffs that year though the team was decent—some would say mediocre.

Mediocrity isn't any fun in sports. And when you really think about it, we don't like mediocre anything—cooking, service, or products. We especially dislike mediocrity when it comes to things that matter. Do you want a mediocre pilot in the cockpit of your airplane or a mediocre surgeon?

I think mediocrity is a sin. Proverbs 18:9 says, "Whoever is slack in his work is a brother to him who destroys." First Corinthians 10:31 says, "So, whether you eat or drink, of whatever you do, do all to the glory of God."

If you are a Christian and you do mediocre work, it diminishes your influence and hurts the cause of Christ. I once asked Duke University professor and researcher, Dr. Harold Koenig, how a believer could succeed in an environment when others were hostile toward their faith? He said, "Focus on doing a really good job." Do what you do well, or don't bother doing it at all.

Back to the Story

Second Kings 24:14 reveals King Nebuchadnezzar's plan of attack for Judah. "He carried away all Jerusalem and all the officials and all the mighty men of valor, 10,000 captives, and all the craftsmen and the smiths. None remained, except the poorest people of the land."

Nebuchadnezzar took these young men as a way of controlling Judah. Rather than using a large occupying force, Nebuchadnezzar would weaken the nation he conquered by removing their talented and intelligent population thereby using them to strengthen his own kingdom. In addition, the youth became quasi-hostages, a message to those left behind to cooperate since the regime had their children.[16]

Daniel 1:3-4 says, "Then the king commanded Ashpenaz, his chief eunuch, to bring some of the people of Israel, both of the royal family and of the nobility, youths without blemish, of good appearance and skillful in all wisdom, endowed with knowledge, understanding learning, and competent to stand in the king's palace, and <u>to teach them the literature and language of the Chaldeans</u>."

The Babylonians chose Daniel, Hananiah, Mishael, and Azariah because they were young men of excellence. They were deemed to have aptitude so they could be taught the literature and language of the Chaldeans. It has been noted by many that the Chaldean language may have been the most difficult language there was to learn in their day. Though they had prepared themselves to serve in the King of Judah's court, God was preparing them for Babylon. The abilities and knowledge they possessed were not developed in a day. It takes time to learn languages and comprehend literature. Apparently, they took advantage of the academic opportunities that came their way, which would later enable them to fulfill God's will for their lives.

How Do Our Youth Excel?

The sluggard does not plow in the autumn; he will seek at harvest and have nothing.
Proverbs 20:4

To survive in a corrupt culture a young person will need a solid spiritual foundation. To thrive, they will strive to be a person of substance. This means our youth need to take advantage of the opportunities that come their way. Success doesn't just happen. They may say: But I attend a bad school. Or I don't have enough money for books. Or we don't have those kinds of resources where we live. While that may be true—along with a host of other facts—everyone is given opportunities and talents and gifts of various shapes and sorts. The key is to use rather than squander whatever opportunities they are given.

Be in the habit of asking your children: What opportunities do you have? What talents do you possess? How can you use those for your good and God's glory?

As a parent, remember you are not in this alone. You are called upon to faithfully prepare the young people entrusted to you. At the same time it is God who is working in their lives to develop them into the person He wants them to be (Philippians 1:6).

Encourage your youth to think about how God is working in them. We see this in the lives of Daniel, Hananiah, Mishael, and Azariah. Though they had prepared themselves well, and were faithful to refuse to defile themselves (Daniel 1:8), it was God who gave them the ability to succeed. In Daniel 1:19-20 we see the result, ". . . among all of them none was found like Daniel, Hananiah, Mishael, and Azariah. Therefore they stood before the king. And in every matter of wisdom and understanding about which the king inquired of them, he found them ten times better than all . . ."

Be Teachable

Help your youth develop a teachable attitude. Nebuchadnezzar only wanted youth that were motivated to learn and willing to invest the time and energy needed to acquire the difficult language of the Chaldeans.

Encourage your youth to seize the opportunity to learn. Never celebrate ignorance. When they realize they do not know something, encourage them to learn about it, and educate themselves. Be quick to discourage them if they brag about what they do not know, as if knowing things is shameful. Try to create an environment where learning is valued, and where youth are encouraged to address their deficiencies.

How are they spending their time?

Activity	Percentage of Time
Study	
Skill acquisition	
Work	
Family	
Friends	
Bible Reading, Worship	
Social Media (Facebook, Twitter)	
Leisure (e.g., Movies, video games)	

Also, just because they can't see themselves using a subject in the future, doesn't mean they will not need it one day. I've heard students exclaim, "I'll never need Algebra!" They planned to be slack about the subject not knowing it will be on most college entrance exams regardless of their major.

I did the same thing. When I was young I thought, "I'll never need Spanish," and did not apply myself even though I took two years of Spanish. Today, I see Spanish speakers daily. At times, I've been alone in Spanish speaking countries unable to communicate. I squandered that opportunity and have lived to regret it. You may have similar experiences you can share with them.

Still, it is best that our youth really apply themselves to the subjects and tasks they enjoy because the more time they spend on something the better they tend to be at it. As they consider things they would like to study and do more, help them consider the way in which they are smart.

God may not expect them to obtain higher education or to be in the top of their class. But He does expect them to use what He has given them. In Matthew 25:14-30 we find the parable of the talents. One man was given five talents, another two, and another just one talent. In the story, Jesus explains that the master's key concern was what they did with their talents. Two of the three workers multiplied their talents. However, the man with only one talent failed to put it to use and was called a "wicked and slothful servant!" Ouch! From the parable we derive the principle "use it or lose it." God expects people to use whatever they have, so help youth to develop a mindset that values learning and wisdom. Apparently, Daniel, Hananiah, Mishael, and Azariah took advantage of the learning opportunities that came their way. They did not sit idly by consumed with boredom, and they were ready when they arrived in Babylon.

Boredom Is Not an Option

This means our youth should never be bored. Wijinand van Tilburg, a psychologist at the University of Southampton, spent some time studying boredom. He concluded that boredom signals that what someone is doing at that moment seems to be lacking purpose.

People who are highly prone to boredom tend to perform poorly on tasks that require sustained attention, and it has been noted that chronic boredom can look a lot like depression.

Strangely, the number of young people who say they are bored is on the rise. This is the case even though it is rare today to be at a point where people do not have anything to do. Our youth are bombarded by stimuli at their fingertips and can resort to television or other screens to alleviate boredom. In many ways their electronic devices contribute to this problem by making them more likely to turn to these electronic devices rather than their own activities when they have a moment with nothing to do. Encourage your children to always have a project, something that stimulates their mind, a book they are reading, a language they are learning, a piece they are writing that they can begin work on when they have a few spare moments. Encourage them to keep a little notebook in their back pocket and be prepared to spring into action when they have spare moments (e.g., stuck in line or traffic, waiting for a late plane or a tardy teacher). I was once stuck in an elevator briefly. Some people panic in such situations. I pulled out my notebook and went to work. It helped me stay calm and gave me a few uninterrupted moments to work. You probably have similar experiences you can share. Teach your youth to take advantage of these moments. Let it never be said of them that they are bored. The research indicates that the bored are more likely to abuse drugs, gamble, and overeat. Even worse, a study of British civil servants indicated that those who experienced a great deal of boredom were more likely to die young than those who were more engaged with the world! It was hypothesized that boredom leads people to take risks.[17] I doubt that Daniel, Hananiah, Mishael, and Azariah spent much time being bored. Instead, I suspect they spent their time developing skills. Our youth can do that too. Rather than being bored, help them focus on developing a specific skill or expanding their knowledge of an area.

Academic Development

Daniel 1:17 says, "As for these four youths, God gave them learning and skill in all literature and wisdom, and Daniel had understanding in all visions and dreams." This Scripture literally says these four were knowers of knowledge. These guys worked hard and took advantage of the skills God gave them. As you interact with young people encourage them to always take the more rigorous classes, read the harder books, and spend more time studying. Help them do what they can to take advantage of the academic opportunities that arise. Also, encourage them to acquire skills, and learn how to do as much as they can. One day they will need that and much more.

Arguably this knowledge saved the lives of these four as recorded in Daniel 2. Nebuchadnezzar was beginning the second year of his kingdom in March or April of 603 B.C., when he asked the wise men to interpret a dream he'd had. In Daniel 2, King Nebuchadnezzar ordered that all of the wise men of Babylon be destroyed (Daniel 2:12). Arioch, the captain of the king's guard began to seek out the wise men. He came to Daniel to kill him. Perhaps Arioch liked Daniel, or realized his value; at any rate, he did not immediately kill him. In fact, he paused and shared with Daniel the problem and allowed Daniel to ask the king to give him some time to work on the interpretation of the dream (Daniel 2:14-16).

Perhaps the ability Hananiah, Mishael, and Azariah had led Nebuchadnezzar to offer them a second chance after they refused to bow down to his golden image before he had them thrown into the fiery furnace. He questioned them (Daniel 3:14), and then gave Hananiah, Mishael, and Azariah another chance to bow down to the image, which they refused (Daniel 3:16-23) resulting in them being thrown into the fiery furnace.

Later, in Daniel 4 we see that Nebuchadnezzar had a problem, a dream he did not understand. After some time they brought Daniel to him. As Daniel walked in he exclaimed, "At last Daniel" when Daniel appeared (Daniel 4:8). Daniel possessed a God-given skill of dream interpretation. It is likely that Hananiah, Mishael, and Azariah also possessed God-given skills like administration. This competence, which God gave them and they faithfully developed, put them into a position to serve and help the people of Babylon. Remember, God has endowed our youth as well with certain knowledge, and areas that they would prefer to work in. Take some time to consider the way in which your youth are smart.

They may not have the ability to interpret dreams or the gift of administration but God has given them certain skills, or talents they need to develop. I fear we think too often of skills and intelligence as characteristics that are only useful in school settings. It may help to examine our youth with a theory of multiple intelligences developed years ago by Harvard psychologist Howard Gardner. He said every person is a unique blend of eight intelligences, and that people are intelligent in different ways.

Linguistic Intelligence: The ability to learn new languages and to use language. People with strengths in this area are good persuaders or storytellers and excel in occupations like writing, poetry, journalism, politics, and law.

Logical-Mathematical Intelligence: The capacity to analyze problems and carry out mathematical operations. The ability to detect patterns, reason deductively, and think logically. People with strengths in this area excel in science, research, mathematics, computer programming, accounting, and engineering.

Bodily-Kinesthetic Intelligence: The ability to control and coordinate complex physical movements. People with strengths in this area may be good at sports, acting, and gymnastics. People with strengths in this area excel in professions where balance and coordination are important like firefighting.

Visual-Spatial Intelligence: The ability to perceive objects in space and know where they should go. People with strengths in this area may be sculpturers, architects, navigators, interior designers, and engineers.

Interpersonal Intelligence: This is the capacity to understand others. People who excel in this area may become teachers, counselors, salespeople, marketing executives, and politicians.

Intrapersonal Intelligence: This is the ability to understand oneself. Writers and philosophers tend to excel in this area.

Musical Intelligence: The ability to work with patterns, rhythms, and sounds. People with strengths in this area are good at singing and playing instruments, and remembering melodies. They excel in professions as musicians, composers, and music teachers.

Naturalistic Intelligence: This is the ability to relate to the natural environment. People who excel in this area often work as farmers or in mining or other outdoor activities.[18]

They could take an assessment at www.miresearch.org, which has been helpful in identifying the type of intelligence people possess. They can also explore their type at www.makeymakey.com.

Whatever their type of intelligence may be, remember it is the intelligence that God has given them. Therefore, encourage them to commit to being a good steward of it. Help them look for ways to expand their knowledge with pertinent books, podcasts, and apps. Find the area where they tend to be the most intelligent and look for more activities they can do in these areas. They should begin by honing their skills and building their aptitude. Help them to develop into a knower of knowledge and develop a skill set that can solve problems.

Challenge them to be a good steward of the opportunities God has given them.

However, to really excel in a particular area they will need to do some hard things like studying and working when others are asleep, playing, or wasting time. They must be a lifelong learner, or they will not impact their culture.

The 10,000-Hour Rule

In his book, *Outliers,* Malcolm Gladwell chronicles the 10,000-hour rule by examining various individuals who have succeeded in remarkable ways. He emphasized how these individuals were prepared at a time when the environment was ripe for them to succeed. He chronicles the preparation of Bill Gates. Bill Gates attended a school where there was a computer club at a time when most colleges did not even have computer clubs. He reportedly "lived" in the computer room. Later he was given access to a computer center developed by programmers at the nearby University of Washington. He could walk to the University of Washington and use the computers at night and did so frequently between the hours of 3:00 and 6:00 a.m. When Gates dropped out of Harvard his sophomore year to start a software company, he'd been programming for 7 years. He had 10,000 hours of experience. He was prepared when the window of opportunity opened.[19] Today it can be hard to get youth to persist at a task (e.g., playing an instrument, math), but this is necessary to become skilled at that task. Help your youth realize that they must spend a lot of time working on a task to succeed, and at times, that will feel a lot like work.

Don't Entertain Excuses

Think back to the incident of Nebuchadnezzar's dream problem (Daniel 2) that we examined earlier. What led Nebuchadnezzar to get angry enough to order the killing of the wise men? Perhaps he had an anger control problem. Probably, but I think his anger was triggered by the behavior of the Chaldeans. The Chaldeans were the political and religious gurus of their day. They were like the people you see on the cable news shows that seem to have all the answers. They could really put on a good show too. However, they were all fluff with no real stuff, and King Nebuchadnezzar wasn't fooled. Daniel 2:4, 8 reads, "Then the Chaldeans said to the king in Aramaic, 'O king, live forever! Tell your servants the dream, and we will show the interpretation.'...The king answered and said, 'I know with certainty that you are trying to gain time.'" The king did not care about symbolism; he had a need that could not be met with symbolism. Though many in our culture believe "image is everything," when problems arise, people get tired rather quickly of excuses and big shows.

> *The Chaldeans answered the king and said,*
> *"There is not a man on earth who can meet*
> *the king's demand, for no great and powerful king*
> *has asked such a thing....The thing*
> *that the king asks is difficult..."*
> Daniel 2:10-11

I think the second reason Nebuchadnezzar became so angry was that the Chaldeans quit quickly. When the Chaldeans could not figure the dream out that they made excuses ("the thing the king asks is difficult") instead of pushing further for answers or searching for someone to assist.

We can learn from this error. When our youth encounter a difficult problem, instead of focusing on why something can't be done, it is better to stop and think: How *can* this be done? Think: problem, alternatives, and solution. What needs to be done? How can it be done? What can they do to work through obstacles? Attack the problem like Daniel. Daniel asked for some time to look into the problem and asked God to help him. Remember, the same God who helped Daniel helps our children.

So instead of building their life around symbolism or fluff, help them prepare to be a problem solver. Encourage them to acquire knowledge and develop skills that can be used to solve real problems in the future. That's the only way they will be prepared to impact the culture.

Grit

You might say the Chaldeans quit too easily because they lacked grit. Our culture also lacks grit. This is clear from studies of children of immigrants. According to a John

See Angela Lee Duckworth discuss Grit: The Key to Success www.ted.com/talks/angela_ lee_duckworth_the_key_to_ success_grit.html

Hopkins University study that tracked nearly 11,000 children, the best students (who later became the most successful young adults) were born in foreign countries and came to the United States before reaching their teens.[20] As these students become more like our culture, they become less successful. One culprit seems to be a lack of grit.

Grit is defined as hard work, dedication, and perseverance that lead people to stick with a goal for years or decades until they succeed. It is an ingredient that predicts success ranging from who succeeds in the National Spelling Bee to the success of cadets at West Point and those who complete Special Forces Training. People who have grit do not mind working very hard. They are not worried about what they could be doing instead of working.[21] They keep at a thing until the job is done.

Are they tougher than a 60-year-old?

In a recent study, teens, 20-somethings, and older adults were asked to rate how tired they felt on a scale of 0 to 6. Americans aged 65 and older reported being less tired than older teens and young 20-somethings. Though the researchers could not determine why this was the case, they hypothesized that this is linked to the influence of technology.[22] It appears that the ease at which many tasks can be performed today has led younger people to be more susceptible to quitting when a task becomes difficult. Keep this vulnerability in mind as you try to assist youth to develop grit.

If our youth are going to be part of a faith that is increasingly unpopular they better have some grit, knowledge and skills that make them valuable. People are more likely to tolerate them if they possess knowledge that can help them as we will see later in the lives of Daniel, Hananiah, Mishael, and Azariah. Remember, God knows the challenges that are coming their way so help your children take advantage of the opportunities He has given them.

Social Development

In addition to preparing by developing their skills and acquiring knowledge to influence the culture, they will need some success working with people. When teaching my students about intellectual assessment, I often give them a hypothetical vignette where they choose a neurosurgeon to remove a brain tumor. In this hypothetical example, the student somehow knows the IQs of the surgeons. I ask, "If you could choose between a neurosurgeon with a 120 IQ and one with 165, which would you choose?" Immediately, my students say, "It depends. How well does the surgeon listen to me? How capable is he or she under pressure? How well does he or she adapt when a situation doesn't go as planned?"

Quickly it becomes obvious that whichever surgeon has the highest IQ is irrelevant. A 120 IQ will do the job intellectually. But, it will be social and emotional competence that provides the added benefit.

Unfortunately, many possess academic knowledge and skill, yet are ineffective because they have not prepared themselves socially. An example is the work of Lewis Terman, who followed 1,470 children into adulthood as they grew up in the San Francisco Bay area in the early 1900s. These children had IQs that ranged from 140-200, a score better than 99 percent of the people those instruments were normed on. Terman expected his students to succeed in remarkable ways. However, he was largely disappointed. These bright people were no more successful than the general population. There were some who were extremely successful, some that were moderately successful, and some that would be considered a failure. It did not turn out at all as Terman had expected.

In his book, *Outliers*, Malcolm Gladwell looked at Terman's work and noted that those who succeeded excelled academically as well as socially.[23] It was social competence (the ability to get along with and work well with others) that made the difference in their lives.

Put the Best Foot Forward

Appearance is a major aspect of social competence. My own experience tells me that how a person appears is very important. I've noted the importance of appearance for students who interview for selective programs at my university. I frequently see a student before an interview team interviews them. Most of the time an applicant that comes to an interview with a sloppy appearance does not get admitted. It is often assumed that they do not take the process seriously. There is a tendency to associate appearance with maturity and capability. Whether our youth like it or not, how they look is important.

Encourage your youth to notice how successful people dress. What does successful dress look like? Note how the president, CEO's, government leaders, and most major college coaches dress or the top achievers in particular fields. We all should dress for the part we want to play.

Notice the description of Daniel and his friends: "Youths without blemish, of good appearance and skillful in all wisdom" (Daniel 1:4a). And again later in that chapter: "Then let our appearance and the appearance of the youths who eat the king's food be observed by you, and deal with your servants according to what you see" (verse 13). Their appearance was important; it left an impression.

Joseph is another example from the Old Testament. When Joseph learned from prison that he would be going to meet Pharaoh, he immediately addressed his appearance to put his best foot forward. "Then Pharaoh sent and called Joseph, and they quickly brought him out of the pit. And when he had shaved himself and changed his clothes, he came in before Pharaoh" (Genesis 41:14).

So, encourage your youth to look nice, neat, and modest. Get them to go to iTunes U, type "Dress for Success" in the search feature, and listen to some of the podcasts from college career centers on dressing well.

Act Well

Daniel 1:4b says that Daniel and his friends were "<u>competent to stand in the king's palace</u>," meaning they understood how to behave in the king's presence and palace. A certain decorum was required to stand or work in the king's palace; they understood and respected that. There is something to being able to act the part. Decorum is not valued as much today as in previous times.

Consider the decorum required for those who visit the *Tomb of the Unknown Soldier* in Arlington, Virginia. An example can be seen in the incident where a 30 year-old woman stood before a sign at the *Tomb of the Unknown Soldier*, and photographed herself in an act of disrespect and posted it on Facebook.[24] The photo resulted in outrage and placed the woman's job in jeopardy.

In many ways, some people no longer know how to act. There is an atmosphere of increased rudeness and insensitivity toward others. In one poll, 79 percent of respondents

> **Netiquette**
>
> www.Netmanners.com
> Netiquette resources: tinyurl.com/25qll
> www.businessemailetiquette.com
> Miss Netiquette's Guide to Twitter:
> tinyurl.com/cyzb25u

said that a lack of respect and incivility is a serious problem in America. Sixty-one percent said it is getting worse.[25]

Teach your youth to be very careful about posts and pictures placed on Facebook, Pinterest, and Instagram. Also, ask them to think twice before tweeting, and to be wise about social media. Get them in the habit of asking themselves: "How would I like for a future employer or admission counselor to see that?" before posting. Sometimes the damage is not done by what they put on their own social media site, but it is the posts, comments, and pictures by their friends that can cause trouble.

College counselors with whom I work often recommend www.socioclean.com to students as they prepare to apply for jobs. This program analyzes social media sites and flags items potential employers might deem as offensive and therefore damage career prospects.

However, in the digital age, once something is out, it can never be completely deleted. So encourage them to think twice before they send that angry email, post that picture, or write their political manifesto.

Who Gets Sued?

In his book, *Blink*, Malcolm Gladwell described the types of doctors who are sued by their patients. Surprisingly, a mistake made by the doctor is not the best predictor. Patients don't sue their doctors if they like them, even if they make mistakes. Most patients sue their doctors because they believe the doctor has bad bedside manners. How do doctors become liked by their patients? Doctors, who appear to care and have time for their patients, enjoy a better relationship with patients.

Medical researcher Wendy Levison looked at the conversations between doctors and their patients. She found that surgeons, who had never been sued, spent an average of three minutes longer with their patients than those who were sued (18.3 minutes versus 15 minutes). Taking their time with patients and giving them just three more minutes saved millions of dollars in malpractice suits.[26] Being liked can be very helpful.

Be Likeable

> And God gave Daniel <u>favor and compassion</u> in the
> sight of the chief of the eunuchs.
> Daniel 1:9

Go back to the beginning of this story when King Nebuchadnezzar prescribed the diet that would have defiled Daniel, Hananiah, Mishael, and Azariah (Daniel 1). It appears from the beginning that these youth were liked. In fact, the Scripture says God gave Daniel this favor with his supervisors. Though they may be different from others it is important to remember that God is working not only in their life but in the life of others to accomplish His will. Proverbs 21:1 says, "The king's heart is a stream of water in the hand of the Lord; he turns it wherever he will." If our children will be faithful to the Scripture God will use them. Note that when Daniel had the problem with the diet he requested to be relieved of the requirement to eat the king's prescribed diet. The supervisor denied his request. Then Daniel went to another and approached him with a solution. In many ways Daniel was already applying Matthew 18 (the passage on dealing with conflict), before it had been written. Though Daniel's initial request was rejected, he ultimately achieved his objective. Daniel was not trying to be confrontational, and he does not appear to have talked badly about his superiors or tried to embarrass them. He appears to have asked privately.

This is a good model for dealing with teachers, principals, college professors, and future employers. Our youth must treat these people with respect, even when they disagree with them. They can use the Daniel model by first discussing a problem privately (also seen in Matthew 18) with the people involved. It is best to always ask: What do I want, and how might it be achieved? Daniel developed a solution that inconvenienced himself ("We will eat water and bread") rather than anyone else. He provided one of his superiors with a solution and achieved his objective. The situation worked out.

Developing Cultural Competences

Daniel, Hananiah, Mishael, and Azariah worked with individuals from many different backgrounds. Daniel 1:21 tells us they were in Babylon until the first year of King Cyrus, meaning they served under many different administrations: Nebuchadnezzar, Belshazzar, Darius, and Cyrus. The cultural competence of these four is seen in Daniel's service to multiple administrations from different nationalities. In order to survive and thrive in these different administrations these four had to successfully work with a variety of people. When Daniel, Hananiah, Mishael, and Azariah were taken to Babylon they were not just leaving their home behind. They were thrust into an environment filled with people that were very different from them.

Look back to the story in Daniel 3 when Nebuchadnezzar built a great statue and he brought those under his control to bow down to it. When Nebuchadnezzar held his ceremony to display his image, Daniel 3:2 notes that "King Nebuchadnezzar sent to gather the satraps, the prefects, and the governors, the counselors, the treasurers, the justices, the magistrates, and all the officials of the provinces to come to the dedication of the image." At this point in history, Nebuchadnezzar had conquered several countries. Many scholars believe the purpose of this endeavor was for Nebuchadnezzar to make sure all of these groups were under his authority. Daniel 3:4 says all "peoples, nations, and languages" bowed down. This indicates that these four regularly interacted with people from different races and nationalities. The Chaldeans noted that Hananiah, Mishael, and Azariah did not bow down to the image and in Daniel 3:12 said, "There are certain Jews whom you have appointed over the affairs of the province of Babylon: Shadrach, Meshach, and Abednego." Since Hananiah, Mishael, and Azariah were leaders in Babylon, they must have been quite effective working with different groups of people. Daniel too possessed this ability, which will become even more obvious later as Daniel will serve under Darius the king of Persia, the nation that will defeat Babylon. Our youth also need this ability. How culturally competent are they? What do they know about various cultures or different groups of people?

Rate Their Cultural Competence
- They view people that look/speak/believe different than they as "those people."

- They are unconcerned with understanding people that look/speak/believe different than they.
- They are unconcerned with getting along with people that look/speak/believe different than they.

If they would answer yes, to any of these statements they need some help. Remind youth that they have far more in common with someone who is a believer even though they may look very different from them. It is important to view all people as important if they hope to reach out to them and help them. If they are unconcerned about getting to know people that are different from them, they are failing to answer God's call to love their neighbor as themselves.

How can they grow in the area of cultural competence? Encourage them to think about how people in a particular culture feel when certain events transpire. Consider what they would say to people from different cultures. Help them seek opportunities to interact with and learn from different cultures, and try to put themselves in the shoes of others to refrain from saying things that might be hurtful. If someone from a different culture seems offended by something they say, rather than becoming defensive, help your child see the issue from the other persons perspective.

It should be noted that when it comes to cultural competence, we tend to overrate our ability. We all probably need to improve in this area. This is a very important area that our children must excel in if they are to positively impact the culture. When we talk about being culturally sensitive, some people protest and say they have no desire to be politically correct. We're not concerned with political correctness, but we want to make sure we are spiritually correct. Fortunately, the Scripture gives us great guidance about how to increase our cultural competence.

Consider the admonition of the Apostle Paul: "If possible, so far as it depends on you, live peaceably with all" (Romans 12:18). What does this mean? How was Paul culturally competent? First Corinthians 9:19-23 explains, "For though I am free from all, I have made myself a servant to all, that I might win more of them. To the Jews I became as a Jew... .To those under the law I became as one under the law... .To those outside the law I became as one outside the law... .To the weak I became weak... . <u>I have become all things to all people, that by all means I might save some</u>. I do it all for the sake of the gospel, that I may share with them in its blessings."

Note that Paul took on the perspective of others so that he could positively influence them. Paul admonished us to respect our leaders and he himself was successful in reaching many in Caesar's household (Philippians 4:22).

As a general principle, it is best for our youth to think about what they are trying to accomplish before they make statements that might offend someone. They need to be especially careful when it comes to political views. Political views can be very polarizing. Encourage your children to be very careful before they disparage a particular candidate or public official. Though they may have the right to do so it is important for them to remember how they are trying to influence people toward Christ. Proverbs 18:19 indicates, "A brother offended is more unyielding than a strong city, and quarreling is like the bars of a castle." Some of the hard teachings of the gospel can be offensive enough (e.g., Jesus is the only way to heaven) without them contributing their own idiosyncrasies. So encourage your children to try to avoid offending people about less important matters. Before they speak they need to ask: Will this statement or argument impede my ability to witness to certain groups of people?

The Culturally Competent Apostle

Consider how the cultural competence of the Apostle Paul enabled him to work with all kinds of very different people. In Acts 13:43 we see Paul ministering to Jews, ". . . many Jews and devout converts to Judaism followed Paul and Barnabas, who, as they spoke with them, urged them to continue in the grace of God." Later in Acts 16, we find Paul answering the call to minister to pagan Europeans in Macedonia. He ministered to leaders like the Philippian Jailor (Acts 16:25-34), as well as the cultural elite (Acts 17:22-34) in his day. When Paul addressed the Areopagus at Athens, it was akin to walking onto a college campus and speaking to the professors in an assembly. Paul ministered to Jewish leaders (Acts 24:24-27; Acts 25-26), military leaders (Acts 27:43), and the wealthy (Philemon). Paul also admonished us to respect government leaders, though ironically it appears one of those leaders ordered his death. Later in Philippians 4:22 we see that even members of Caesar's household became believers.

So teach them not to attack someone (teachers, principals, professors, employers, government leaders) just because everyone else does. It is also wise to refrain from attacking an easy target or someone who is particularly unpopular at the moment. It doesn't tend to garner the respect of others. Their conversation will be very different from their peers as Colossians 4:6 teaches, "Let your speech always be gracious, seasoned with salt, so that you may know how you ought to answer each person." As they deal with others we want them to be honest, but wise. Always keeping the big idea in mind. Being kind and having time for others will give them the opportunity to influence others toward Christ. We are trying to reach people with the gospel, and it helps to be liked.

Emotional Development

Intellectual competence and social competence are necessary to influence the culture. However, our youth will not achieve their objectives without emotional maturity. Are they easily disappointed? Do they find themselves especially sensitive to criticism? Are they fearful?

Daniel Goleman's classic book, *Working with Emotional Intelligence*, was derived by analyzing what more than 120 companies wanted in their employees. Sixty-seven percent of the competencies desired were emotional in nature. He defines emotional competence as self-awareness (knowledge of your own abilities and shortcomings), self-regulation (able to manage emotional distress), motivation (goal oriented and able to overcome setbacks), empathy (aware of how others think and feel), and social skills (able to work well with other people). Business leaders indicated a desire for employees who listened well, were able to get past setbacks, were motivated, were able to get along well with others, and were willing to contribute to others.[27]

How do they see themselves?

Some people encounter difficulty and begin to falter. There may come a time when your children see themselves as a failure. If they are struggling, it will be important to engage in an activity called story editing. For example, in a situation where college students have performed poorly in their first year of study, those who have read articles about students who performed poorly initially, but improved over time tend to do so as well. This seemed to especially be the case when the students wrote out a narrative that described how they would do better once they learned the ropes. So if your youth struggle you might encourage them to journal about how that is to be expected and that they will do better once they get your feet on the ground.[28] Don't you think Daniel, Hananiah, Mishael, and Azariah did something like that? They were exiles of Judah, however, they must have seen themselves as prophets to the Babylonian kingdom or something else, which led to their success.

Be Calm

The emotional competence of Daniel, in particular, has been seen in the incident from Daniel 2 when Nebuchadnezzar ordered the killing of the wise men because the Chaldeans were unable to tell Nebuchadnezzar his dream. Daniel 2:13-14 says, "So the decree went out, and the wise men were about to be killed; and they sought Daniel and his companions, to kill them. Then <u>Daniel replied with prudence and discretion to Arioch</u>, the captain of the king's guard, who had gone out to kill the wise men of Babylon."

Daniel, Hananiah, Mishael, and Azariah had to be cool and calm under pressure. Not only did they survive the traumatic overthrow of their nation and subsequently stand up for their beliefs regarding diet, but they also, encountered a death threat when King Nebuchadnezzar was upset because the wise men could not interpret his dream (Daniel 2:13). Daniel, Hananiah, Mishael, and Azariah were considered wise men. Nebuchadnezzar ordered their execution. When someone visits you with the task of killing you, well, that can elevate your stress level. Note that Daniel replied with "prudence and discretion" (Daniel 2:14), and calmly asked, "why is this so urgent?" (Daniel 2:15). Daniel slowed this crisis down by asking Arioch a question. He also asked that he be given some time to work on the problem. Arioch allowed Daniel to make his request to the king and Daniel was given more time to work on an answer to the dream (Daniel 2:16). Next, Daniel enlisted the help of his godly friends (Hananiah, Mishael, and Azariah), and they prayed about the problem (Daniel 2:17-18). God gave Daniel the dream and its interpretation (Daniel 2:19). Daniel used the situation as an opportunity to tell Nebuchadnezzar about the one true God ("There is a God in heaven who reveals mysteries." Daniel 2:28). A crisis became an opportunity, and Daniel and his friends were catapulted forward (Daniel 2:48-49).

We can learn from this event. When our youth find themselves in danger, they need to slow things down. This allows them to calm down a bit and to think about an appropriate course of action. Similarly, if they can be cool during a crisis they will find that many of these crises become opportunities to help and influence others.

To succeed they will need to learn to deal well with stress and pressure. As parents, allow your children to be in stressful situations so they can learn how to deal with them well. As they do, their emotional intelligence should grow.

Another example of emotional intelligence is in Daniel 5 in the famous story of the handwriting on the wall. Nebuchadnezzar is no longer on the scene. He has been replaced by King Belshazzar who is throwing a big feast with thousands of people (Daniel 5:1). He is using vessels that Nebuchadnezzar had taken from the temple in Jerusalem. This was very disrespectful to the God of Daniel. During the party, the king became very frightened as a finger began to write on the wall (Daniel 5:5-6). Daniel is not at this party. It appears that he is not held with the same esteem that he experienced in the kingdom of Nebuchadnezzar. One of the big tests of emotional intelligence is in how a person deals with disappointment and those who devalue them. Instead of pouting over these apparent slights, Daniel prepared to help when he was called to assist Belshazzar. How can we deal with disappointment or being devalued? The passage in Daniel 5 reinforces the principle that people will eventually seek out the help of those who are competent once the situation gets desperate enough.

Bad things will happen to our youth so they must be prepared to deal with them. The Word of God will be a comfort to them, and they will need to develop techniques like walking, exercising, or praying to help them cope. Our children must learn to deal with discouragement, which is a key to emotional competence.

Spiritual Development

Academic, social, and emotional competences are necessary. However, competence begins with the Lord. Proverbs 1:7 says, "The fear of the LORD is the beginning of knowledge; fools despise wisdom and instruction."

We have already discussed how Daniel, Hananiah, Mishael, and Azariah must have read the Hebrew Bible and its prominence in their prayer life. But it is important to note that those who knew them acknowledged that they were spiritually mature.

Nebuchadnezzar spent enough time with Daniel to know he was spiritually mature. In Daniel 4, another dream Nebuchadnezzar had is recorded. We will look at this closer later but it alarmed Nebuchadnezzar (Daniel 4:5). The Chaldeans were unable to give the answer to the dream so Nebuchadnezzar turned to Daniel. When Daniel arrived, Daniel 4:8 records the king's words, "At last Daniel came in before me—he who was named Belteshazzar after the name of my god, and in whom is the spirit of the holy gods—and I told him the dream." Nebuchadnezzar, a prideful and oppressive man, even saw the spiritual competence of Daniel. He still called him Daniel (meaning, "God is Judge") though he noted he had changed his name.

Decades later, Nebuchadnezzar's wife spoke about Daniel as the nation faced another crisis: "There is a man in your kingdom <u>in whom is the spirit of the holy gods</u>. In the days of your father, light and understanding and wisdom like the wisdom of the gods were found in him, and King Nebuchadnezzar, your father—your father the king—made him chief of the magicians, enchanters, Chaldeans, and astrologers" (Daniel 5:11).

Even Daniel's enemies recognized his faith. They realized his faith was the only thing they could use against him if they wished to attack him: "Then these men said, 'We shall not find any ground for complaint against this Daniel <u>unless we find it in connection with the law of his God</u>'" (Daniel 6:5).

After his faith was used against him, Darius too, described Daniel's faith though the ruler cast Daniel into a den of lions: "Then the king commanded, and Daniel was brought and cast into the den of lions. The king declared to Daniel, '<u>May your God, whom you serve continually, deliver you!</u>'" (Daniel 6:16). These spiritual competencies were developed in their youth and served them throughout their lives. Our youth can develop these competencies.

Dr. Robert Picirilli is a modern day example of a spiritually competent person. In the videos linked at survivingculture.com, he first discusses how these competencies helped him early in his life as he committed himself to follow Christ. Later he discussed how these competencies have helped him even as he has transitioned into older age. May our youth too be a man or woman of faith. May they spend time in prayer to God and reading His Word so it is obvious to others they have been with God (Acts 4:13).

Bring it All Together

Model

The parents of Daniel, Hananiah, Mishael, and Azariah as well as the leaders who impacted them were probably nobles in Judah. They likely modeled excellence to these youth. You can help your youth by doing your work with excellence. Demonstrate by your actions your desire to do all to the glory of God.

Teach

The parents of Daniel, Hananiah, Mishael, and Azariah probably spent a lot of time preparing them academically, socially, emotionally, and spiritually as we have already discussed. Though much of the preparation might have been to serve in the kingdom of Judah, what they learned clearly prepared them for Babylon. The point for us is that in addition to spiritual development, we must be very involved in the academic, social, and emotional development of our youth.

Create

The environment that the parents of Daniel, Hananiah, Mishael, and Azariah created likely included opportunities to interact with many of the leaders in Judah. You can create an environment where learning and achievement are honored. You can do this by honoring teachers and leaders and emphasizing the importance of these individuals. Hold youth accountable, and do not allow them to be slack. Also, create an environment where youth can develop emotionally. Visit the sick, attend funerals, allowing your youth to see the good and the bad of life.

Chapter 3

Do They Know How To Be Themselves?

Try to help your children realize God has called them to serve Him, and that the only way to be truly happy in life is to fulfill that calling. God made our youth for a particular purpose.

Ephesians 2:10 says, "We are his workmanship, created in Christ Jesus for good works, which God prepared beforehand, that we should walk in them." This means God has gifted each person to do what He wants them to do. Psalm 139:13-14 says, "For you formed my inward parts, you knitted me together in my mother's womb: I will praise you for I am fearfully and wonderfully made. Wonderful are your works; my soul knows it very well." So God was involved in every detail of every person from their interest, abilities, and desires, all the way down to their DNA. God has prepared them for the task He wants them to perform.

In his book *Creativity,* Mihaly Csikszentmihalyi examined the lives of 91 people who were at the top of their field. These people were known for their creativity. Csikszentmihalyi noted that before one could excel in an area he or she needed to be extremely proficient

See Mihaly Csikszentmihalyi discuss flow at: www.ted.com/talks/mihaly_csikszentmihalyi_on_flow.html

in that content. Today people often think of creativity as something that happens suddenly. Csikszentmihalyi has noted that real creativity is usually the result of years of work. [29]

This observation is similar to the 10,000-hour rule discussed in Chapter 2 that indicates one must spend a lot of time in an area to know it well before arriving at a level of creativity.

God made some of our youth to excel in math. He has endowed them with ability others may not possess. To truly excel and be a good steward of this ability they must take many rigorous courses in mathematics (e.g., geometry, trigonometry, and calculus). Since God made them this way, in addition to coursework, they will be thinking about and doing math when they are not taking classes. They might find themselves thinking about math in their spare time. If their field is history, in addition to coursework, they will probably have history books in their book bag that they will read in their spare time and history podcasts on their MP3 player. This is the 10,000-hour rule at work. To be good, they must spend their time on the things they love to do.

In another book called *Flow*, Csikszentmihalyi discussed happiness. He stated that it is a mistake to pursue happiness itself, and that those who tend to be truly happy are those who engage in activities for enjoyment and satisfaction that totally engage their minds.[30] One might conclude from his work that one will only be truly happy when he or she is engrossed in the activities he or she were created to perform or become the person God has made him or her to be.

The Bible teaches us that if you delight in God He will give you the desires of your heart (Psalm 37:4). What does that mean? It means as a person identifies with Christ as their Lord, their only hope of salvation, that He redeems them, turning their self-centered, sinful desires into a heart, a life that finds its most joy in pursuing God's desires for them. That is when a person settles into what he or she was created to be. God makes them want what He wants them to want.

Step 1. Present Their Life to God

Ask your youth: Is there anything you would not do even if you felt God wanted you to do it? Is there anywhere you would not go even if you felt God wanted you to go there? Romans 12:1 says, "...present your bodies as a living sacrifice, holy and acceptable to God, which is your spiritual worship."

Therefore, the first thing every person must do is to give their life to God with the attitude, "I will go where You want me to go, and do whatever You want me to do." This step cannot be skipped.

Too many people put parameters around God as the Old Testament prophet Jonah did. Apparently, Jonah was willing to serve God, but on his own terms. God instructed Jonah to go to minister to Nineveh (Jonah 1:2). He was unwilling to serve in Nineveh, which was an enemy of Israel, and actually went in the opposite direction (Jonah 1:3). Contrast his attitude with the attitude of Daniel. Daniel prepared to serve in Judah but was called to serve in Babylon (the enemy of Judah). Daniel's love for God and his relationship with God allowed him to serve faithfully in Babylon.

Step 2. Assessment Time

The next step is to conduct a sober or serious assessment upon them. Romans 12:3 says, one should "not think of himself more highly than he ought to think, but to think with sober judgment, each according to the measure of faith that God has assigned." Often, when I have asked college students or young workers why they selected their major or a particular job they say, "That's where the money is" or "My friends suggested it." It would be wiser to choose a field or job because you were made for it. If they are good at something and like it, they are going to excel. It all starts with finding the strengths God has given them.

Find Their Strengths

Help your children find their strengths. The key to success is for a young person to determine what God made them to do and go do it. So it is critical for them to find the strengths God has given them. Help them think of the kind of work they will do or how they will spend their time, ask them: What are you good at? Get them to start by looking at their grades. What are their favorite academic subjects? What academic subjects do they dislike? What is their work history? What are their hobbies? What club and church activities do they most enjoy? Based on their own assessment, what are their top three favorite subjects? What are their least favorite subjects? They cannot ignore the subjects they dislike. In order to be well rounded, they will need a certain level of proficiency in broad areas.

However, once they find they are better suited for certain areas, it is wise to spend more time there. For example, let's say their grades and interest are high in the social study subjects, but they dislike math. It would then be wise to explore these areas by taking as many rigorous courses (e.g., US Government, European History, and Economics) as they can.

> Find free online courses and books of interest to you at www.openculture.com

To get a better understanding of what they are good at take a look at their latest achievement test results. Where did they score the highest? The lowest?

To understand what the scores mean look at two terms. The first is a stanine. These scores help them see how their abilities on certain subjects compare to other students their age. Scores of 1 to 3 indicate that they are not as strong in these areas as other students. Scores of 4 to 6 indicate that they are like most people in these areas. Scores of 7 to 9 indicate that they do better in this area than most people. Another way to understand these scores is to look at the percentile rank (PR). This number tells them specifically how their skill level in an area compares to others. For example, if they score in the 35th percentile on an area, this means they did as well as or better than 35 percent of the norming population on this instrument. This would mean this area is not a strength for them. On the other hand, if they scored in the 65th percentile (as well as or better than 65 percent of the norming population), this would be a strength for them. Also, look at the scaled scores, which can help them monitor their progress from one year to another.

Looking for an Aptitude Test?
PSAT: www.CollegeBoard.com
SAT: www.SAT.CollegeBoard.org
ACT: www.ACT.org
ASVAB: http://official-asvab.com

When they find themself excelling in an area, encourage them to spend more time in those areas. If their school does not offer courses in some of these subjects, talk to their school counselor or princi-

Looking for AP courses your school does not have?
Go to https://apstudent.collegeboard.org/

pal about them taking some of these courses at a community college or online.

The research indicates that taking high-level mathematics courses like pre-calculus in high school increases the likelihood of success in college. Taking Advanced Placement (AP) or International Baccalaureate courses increases the likelihood of success in college even if students fail the end of course exam. The more of these types of courses taken in high school the more likely a student persists at their four-year or two-year institution. A rigorous high school curriculum is key to success.[31]

You can also assess your youths strengths by looking at aptitude tests like the Preliminary Scholastic Assessment Test (PSAT), Scholastic Assessment Test (SAT), and American College Testing (ACT). These instruments are usually used as a means to enter a program of study, but they too can provide a good indication of their ability. However, these tend to be limited to their verbal, quantitative, and analytical skills. Get them to ask their school counselor about taking the Armed Services Vocational Aptitude Battery (ASVAB). The ASVAB will provide a wider range of skill areas.

Step 3. What are they like?

Psalm 139:15-16 reads, "My frame was not hidden from you, when I was being made in secret, intricately woven in the depths of the earth. Your eyes saw my unformed substance; in your book were written, every one of them, the days that were formed for me, when as yet there was none of them." This indicates that their ability to do things was given to them by the Lord so there will be tasks your youth are better at performing than others because God made them that way. Every person is different with different functions within the body of Christ.

What do they do well with minimal effort? What kind of tasks do they find themselves doing and lose track of time? What are they like?

Now concerning spiritual gifts, brothers, I do not want you to be uninformed. ...For to one is given through the Spirit the utterance of wisdom, and to another the utterance of knowledge according to the same Spirit, to another faith by the same Spirit, to another gifts of healing by the one Spirit, to another the working of miracles, to another prophecy, to another the ability to distinguish between spirits, to another various kinds of tongues, to another the interpretation of tongues. ...And God has appointed in the church first apostles, second prophets, third teachers, then miracles, then gifts of healing, helping, administrating, and various kinds of tongues.
1 Corinthians 12:1, 8-10, 28

Having gifts that differ according to the grace given to us, let us use them: if prophecy, in proportion to our faith; if service, in our serving; the one who teaches, in his teaching; the one who exhorts, in his exhortation; the one who contributes, in generosity;

the one who leads, with zeal; the one who does acts
of mercy, with cheerfulness.
Romans 12:6-8

When I was a boy, I could not understand why I had so much trouble playing baseball. I seemed good at most sports, but when it came to baseball, I could not throw. It bothered me. I had been given a baseball glove and could field well with it; I just could not throw very far. One day I went to my backyard and threw two baseballs. I threw the first ball with my right hand as hard as I could. It did not go far. Then I threw with my left hand. The ball went out of the yard and over a big fence. Soon after, I met a man who lent me a left-handed glove. I had never seen a glove for left-handed people, but that day I realized how liberating it can be to know what you are really good at and be able to do what you were made to do.

In a similar fashion, our youth have a personality, interests, and abilities God gave them when He created them. When they operate in the areas where they are gifted, they tend to be more successful, happier, and more influential.

For example, do they like working with people or would they rather work alone? Do they tend to focus on what could be or are they more concerned with the here and now? Do they make decisions based on logic or find themselves making decisions based on their concerns for someone else? Do they make decisions quickly, or do they feel like they need as much information as possible before coming to a conclusion? It is important to discover the way God made them to be and for them to operate in that realm.

Interests

Some people enjoy working with machinery and working alone while others prefer to be with other people and might even struggle to change the pressure in the tires of a car. These preferences are a result of a person's interests.

Psychologist John Holland studied people and their occupations and concluded that people have interest types, which can be described as realistic, investigative, artistic, social, enterprising, and conventional.

Realistic

People with the realistic type tend to enjoy activities requiring physical, mechanical, and spatial abilities. They prefer concrete rather than abstract tasks. They are often described as quiet and tend to value freedom, ambition, and self-control. They tend to gravitate to occupations such as engineering, navigation, plumbing, and other service occupations like electricians and technicians. Inventors tend to be realistic. Thomas Edison and Mike Rowe are good examples of the realistic type.

Realistic Types[32]

Academic Subjects	Value	Activities	Majors and Programs	Typical Occupations
Math	Quiet	Agricultural clubs	Agriculture	Agriculture
		Intramural Sports	Animal Science	Computer Repair
		ROTC	Automotive Services	Law Enforcement
			Aviation	Military Activity
			Electronics	Outdoors
			Engineering	Transportation
			Forestry	
			Heating, Air Conditioning, and Refrigeration	
			Horticulture	
			Medical Technology	
			Welding	

Get them to rate the strength of their realistic characteristics.

Low   Medium   High

Investigative

Investigative people tend to like science, medicine, mathematics, and research. They are often described as reserved, curious, thorough, analytical, and scholarly. They tend to value wisdom and logic. These people tend to gravitate to occupations in the sciences and occupations that require the highest educational levels. Examples include laboratory technician, computer programmer, and electronics worker. Albert Einstein and Dr. Benjamin Carson are good examples of the investigative type.

Investigative Types[33]

Academic Subjects	Value	Activities	Majors and Programs	Typical Occupations
Science	Curiosity	Chess Club	Anthropology	Engineering
		Science Club (Astronomy, Geology)	Archeology	Health Care
			Biology	Research Science
		Volunteer for research projects	Botany	
			Chemistry	
			Computer Information Systems	
			Health Sciences	
			Mathematics	
			Meteorology	
			Paramedics	
			Social Sciences	
			Zoology	

Get them to rate the strength of their investigative characteristics.

Low   Medium   High

<--->

Artistic

Artistic people tend to like activities involving self-expression, communication, and culture. They are often described as careless, disorderly, dreamy, introspective, sensitive, sophisticated, and creative. They tend to value beauty and imagination. These people tend to gravitate to occupations involving music, writing, and art. T. S. Eliot and Pablo Picasso are good examples of the artistic type.

Artistic Types[34]

Academic Subjects	Value	Activities	Majors and Programs	Typical Occupations
Language classes	Introspection	Foreign Language Clubs	Advertising	Advertising
Art		Musical Group	Architecture	Architecture
Drama		Student Publications	Broadcasting	Culinary Arts
		Theater Productions	Creative Writing	Entertainment
			Design	Writing
			English	Video/Film
			Fine Arts	
			Mass Communication	
			Music	
			Education	

Get them to rate the strength of their artistic characteristics.

Low   Medium   High

< _____ >

Social

Social people tend to like activities involving people, teamwork, and community. They are often described as capable, enthusiastic, friendly, kind, warm, and persuasive. These people tend to gravitate to occupations like teaching and counseling. Leaders tend to be social. Most politicians and pastors are good examples of the social type.

Social Types[35]

Academic Subjects	Value	Activities	Majors and Programs	Typical Occupations
Psychology	Cooperation	Intramural Sports	Child Development	Child Care
Business		Resident Hall Advisor	Counseling	Counseling
		Tutoring	Criminology	Education
		Organizations	Education	Health Care
			Hearing and Speech Sciences	Tourism
			Nursing	Hospitality
			Public Health	
			Recreation	
			Religious Studies	

Get them to rate the strength of their social characteristics.

Low	Medium	High

< _____ >

Enterprising

Enterprising people tend to like activities involving selling, managing, and persuading. They are often described as aggressive, extroverted, and popular. These people tend to gravitate to occupations involving business and politics. Leaders tend to be enterprising; Henry Ford, Andrew Carnegie, and Steve Jobs are good examples of the enterprising type.

Enterprising Type[36]

Academic Subjects	Value	Activities	Majors and Programs	Typical Occupations
Government History	Adventure	Business Student Organizations Campus Political Groups Student Government Association	Business Cosmetology Culinary Training Finance Government History Insurance Management Marketing Political Science Prelaw Public Administration	Business Insurance Investments Legal Services Marketing Management Real Estate Sales

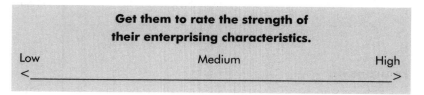

Get them to rate the strength of their enterprising characteristics.

Low   Medium   High

< _____ >

Conventional

Conventional people tend to like organizing, setting up procedures, and keeping records. They are often described as practical, accurate, stable, meticulous, precise, and efficient. These people tend to gravitate to occupations involving data management, accounting, and investing. Experts in finance and commerce tend to be conventional. John D. Rockefeller is a good example of the conventional type.

Conventional Type[37]

Academic Subjects	Value	Activities	Majors and Programs	Typical Occupations
Math	Stability	Financial Aid Advising	Accounting	Accounting
		Office Assistant	Banking	Banking
			Financial Planning	Bookkeeping
		Secretary or Treasurer of a Student Organization	Office Systems	Data Management
		Math or Statistics Tutor	Mathematics Statistics	Office Work Tax Consulting

Get them to rate the strength of their conventional characteristics.

Low   Medium   High

<   >

So what is their type? Help them find out and spend more time on those tasks, being the person God created them to be.

How to find your type
Career Key: www. careerkey.org
Self-Directed Search:
www.self-directed-search.com
Also, consider the Kuder: www.kuder.com

Personality

God also made them with a particular type of personality, and they are more likely to excel if they can work in these areas that allow them to express themself. What kind of personality do they have?

How do you find your type?
See a career counselor to take the Myers-Briggs Type Indicator.
Go online to view the Keirsey:
www. Keirsey.com

It can be helpful to consider four types assessed by an instrument called the Myers-Briggs Type Indicator (MBTI).

If they are in college, they might be able to take the MBTI in their career-counseling center. The MBTI is based on the work of Carl Jung. One's type can also be assessed for a fee using the Keirsey Temperament Sorter (KTS).

Extraversion or Introversion

People tend to be extraverted or introverted. Extraverted people are energized when they work in groups and are able to be with other people. They may like public speaking and occupations like selling and politics. They like activity and tend to talk more than they listen.

Introverts on the other hand do their best work when they are alone or in small groups. If they are working on a project with other people, they will need some down time to get rejuvenated once the project is complete. They like occupations like science and writing or anything involving introspection. They listen more than they talk.

In our culture, introverts are not valued as much as others though our culture needs them.

Preference Types	Occupational Areas[38]
Sensing and Thinking	Surgery, law, accounting, working with machinery
Sensing and Feeling	Nursing, teaching, social work, selling, service jobs
Intuition and Feeling	Teaching, preaching, adverstising, counseling, writing, and research
Intuition and Thinking	Science, computing, mathematics, and finance

Sensing or Intuition

People who are sensing tend to focus on facts and take in information using their five senses. Sensing types are oriented toward the present; they value common sense and practicality.

Intuitive types tend to take in information from patterns and focus on what could be. They value imagination and ingenuity. They tend to be able to read between the lines.

Thinking or Feeling

Thinking types tend to look at things logically and make decisions based on logic. They might say they value truth over tact. Feelers tend to think about the impact of a particular decision.

Feelers tend to be tender minded and subjective.

Sometimes people who are thinkers may be perceived as harsh while feelers might be viewed as a push over.

Judging or Perceiving

Judgers like a planned and organized approach to life. Judgers are quick to make decisions. They tend to be on time and like organization. They want to see things resolved, like fixed deadlines and are product oriented.

Perceivers do not wish to miss anything. They may be late or considered messy and are slower to make a decision. Perceivers like flexibility and prefer to keep their options open. They are process oriented and often miss deadlines. To learn more check out Tieger and Barron-Tieger *Do What You Are*, and Kroeger, and Thueson's *Type Talk at Work*.

A Personal Profile
What are my top 3 academic subjects?

1.
2.
3.

What are my top 3 interest areas?

1.
2.
3.

What is your personality like:

E or I

S or N

T or F

J or P

My Top Occupations

1. _____

Key Tasks Performed: _____

Education & Training Required: _____

2. _____

Key Tasks Performed: _____

Education & Training Required: _____

3. _____

Key Tasks Performed: _____

Education & Training Required: _____

4. _____

Key Tasks Performed: _____

Education & Training Required: _____

5. _____

Key Tasks Performed: _____

Education & Training Required: _____

Step 4: Sum It Up

O*NET is a very helpful website produced by the United States Department of Labor (www.onetonline.org). There your children can explore occupations tied to their personal profile. For example, if their favorite subject is history, they can type "history" in the occupational search slot. Also, get them to select advanced search and knowledge. They can do a similar search by selecting abilities. For example, get them to type in "writing" and look at the occupational choices that are provided. Have them identify occupations that would be of interest to them and explore the tasks performed in this job as well as the skills and education required to perform them. Get them to do the same search again, but this time type their top interest into the occupational search slot and under the advanced search option choose "interest." Get them to try to make a list of ten possible occupations.

Now ask them to go to the Occupational Outlook Handbook (www.bls.gov/ooh), which is also operated

Check out the U.S. Department of Labor website that helps youth match skills to an occupation: http://mynextmove.dol.gov

by the United States Department of Labor. They can explore the occupational groups there (e.g., arts and design, business and financial, healthcare, military, sales). Ask them what core tasks are performed by people in these occupations? What type of training is required for this occupation? If the occupation requires college, what majors are usually required? Is graduate or professional school necessary? Get them to pay special attention to the tasks, condition, location, and benefits of each occupation.

Step 5: How Do They Get There?

Once they narrow down some possible occupations, ask them to consider interviewing some people in those positions. Have them use the questions below as a starting point for the interview:

1. How did you obtain this position?
2. What is a typical day like for you?
3. What do you like most about this position?
4. What do you dislike about this position?
5. What are some of the biggest challenges facing your industry?
6. What professional associations should I be connecting with?
7. How do you see the industry changing over the next 10 years? [39]
8. How did you prepare for this career?
9. What are the opportunities for advancement in this field?

Paying for College

Going 2 College: www.going2college.org
Provides resources to explore, plan, and examine how to pay for college.

College Savings Plans Network:
www.collegesavings.org
Provides strategies for getting financial aid and being admitted into college.

FAFSA Forecaster: www.FAFSA4caster.ed.gov
Examines options for paying for college.

Federal Student Aid: www.studentaid.gov
U.S. Department of Education site where youth can see if they qualify for financial aid and apply for aid.

Choosing a College

College Affordability and Transparency Center:
http://collegecost.gov
U.S. Department of Education site that examines the cost, graduation, and employment rate of colleges.

College Navigator: http://nces.ed.gov/collegenavigator
Institute for Education Sciences site that allows youth to make comparisons between colleges they are considering.

National Survey of Student Engagement:
http://Nsse.iub.edu
Download the NSSE's pocket guide for choosing a college.

Find Training

Should they go to college? I encourage youth to consider going to college even if they choose an occupation that does not require the training. Earning an associate's or bachelor's degree can provide them with opportunities.

As they consider colleges, remind them to remember their goals. They are preparing for a particular occupation to help them be a person of influence.

Do not forget that going to college involves more than getting an education. College is an opportunity to grow and socialization is important as well. They will also be meeting people that will become a network, often friends for life.

Many of them will meet their spouse at college so for that reason I encourage you to strongly consider suggesting a Christian college. Doing so will also help them better prepare, especially if they will be going to graduate or professional school in the future.

Should they go to a big or small college? Often people choose a college for the wrong reason like being a fan of the sports team or having friends who attend the college. You want them to attend a college that will help them grow.

There are many resources that can help them as they choose. The College Navigator website can be used to compare colleges. Look at the class sizes at each school, the completion rate of programs, and the student to faculty ratio, which are important to their success.

Vocational Training

Suppose they are going the non-college route. A vocational education program (www.rvm.org) may work for them or perhaps enlisting in the military (www.todaysmilitary.com). If they are looking at a vocational school, examine the success rate (e.g., percentage to complete, percentage employed upon graduation) of the school. Make sure that the vocational school they are considering is licensed or accredited. They can find accredited schools at the U.S. Department of Education's website: www.ope.ed.gov/accreditation/. They can also find key information about the program they are interested in and compare them to other training programs as well.[40]

Help Them Succeed

The key is whatever a young person is doing, they always need to be learning, whether that involves going to college, technical school, or immediately going into the workforce. Today, many are quick to point out that Steve Jobs, Bill Gates, and Mark Zuckerberg did not finish college. Perhaps they didn't finish but they were certainly learning (as evidenced by the 10,000 hour rule). The fact is that most people cannot acquire the kinds of skills they acquired without some formal training opportunities.

The problem isn't that college is not relevant; the problem is that many have attended college as some kind of rite of passage rather than as an opportunity to acquire skills and develop. The results have been devastating. In 2009, only 57.8 percent of students attending four-year colleges graduated in less than six years, and just 32.9 percent of those in two-year institutions graduated in three years. It should not surprise us that when people list their greatest regrets in life, education seems to be the biggest one.[41] So remind your children when they are thinking of getting slack and skipping a class to remember they are likely to regret that in 10 years (and even in 10 days when they have their mid-term).

Encourage Them Get to Know Their Teachers

The habits developed in school can prepare children for learning throughout their lives. To succeed, it will help for the student to be in the habit of talking to their teachers about their studies. In college, young people who frequently talk to their advisor greatly improve their chances of graduating. In one study, talking to an academic advisor "sometimes" or "often" improved the chances of completion of both four-year and two-year students by as much as 53 percent.[42]

If attending college, it helps to talk to their advisor midway through each semester to select the classes they will take the next semester. Also, they need to meet with him or her if they are having trouble of any kind—struggling with a class, considering dropping a class, and/ or rethinking their major. Youth need to pay attention to the drop deadline for courses and consult with their advisor (and the course instructor) long before that deadline, especially if they are struggling.

"If your knowledge doesn't cumulate, your troubles will." D. J. Foss[43]

They May Fail

It is important for youth to realize they may fail. In research on performance we have

> If they struggle with learning issues, encourage them to take a look at *First Aid for Your Emotional Hurts: Learning Problems*.

learned that youth who understand failure is a possibility are less likely to fail and perform better in school than those who do not think failure can happen.[44] They can expect to encounter great difficulty, and they will need to work hard to succeed.

Get the Most Out of School

Help them get into the habit of becoming familiar with their assignments, and to develop a master calendar with key dates (major projects, papers, and tests). A master schedule will help them stay on track when a whim hits them.[45]

Help them set, achieve, and revise goals about their education and their future. The more specific their goals are the better chance they have of success. For example, instead of setting a goal to make better history grades, help them set a goal like I will spend 20 percent more time (or 3 more hours) studying this week to prepare for a history exam.

It even helps to talk to youth about taking notes in their classes. Instruct them to listen for key phrases like, "the important point here is," "they key is," "as I've said before," and "remember" because this is the material that is usually on the test![46]

Remind them to actively review their notes, which is an important key to studying. The very act of taking a test can also be a learning experience; so tell them to start preparing for their exams on the first day of class.

Their study skills, habits, and attitudes are the top predictors of success. Talk to them about what they actually do when they study. The amount of time spent studying is not actually a good predictor of grades. It helps for a youth to be aware of their present knowledge state and know how far it is from their goal so they can get to where they want to be. Genuine learning occurs when a student studies in a mindful way.[47]

Many youth think that the most effective way to study is to spend a massive amount of time on a subject. However, the research indicates that it is far more effective to spread the learning out over days. For example, five 2-hour sessions distributed over 5 days is superior to two 5-hour sessions concentrated in 2 days. Ten days of 1-hour sessions is better yet. A student will do better if they spend a large amount of their time studying to be tested. This is called the retrieval effect. So give your youth frequent quizzes on the material they are studying. Test taking appears to improve learning in people of all ages.

> "There is no substitute for hard work."
> **Thomas Edison**

However, youth do need time for uninterrupted work so help them find blocks of time for regular study. Also, if they study in the same place all the time they will recall the material better. Remind them not to multitask (surf the internet, respond to texts) when they are studying.[48]

Texting, social networking, and other media have been linked to poor academic performance, in a study of 483 female college freshmen across various forms of media: television, movies, music, surfing the Internet, social networking, talking on a cell phone, texting, reading magazines, newspapers, and playing video games. The participants reported their GPAs and academic confidence behaviors and problems. On average, the women spent nearly half their day engaged in some form of media use, particularly texting, listening to music, surfing the Internet, and social networking. Media use in general was associated with lower GPAs and other negative academic outcomes. On the other hand, newspaper reading and listening to music were linked to positive academic performance.[49]

As your youth read the text for their course, encourage them to try to understand the author's goals, and figure out the main goal and subgoals. It helps if they preview a chapter before reading it. As they read, they will need to find the main points. They should ask themselves questions about what they are reading (the retrieval affect). When they finish,

> **What do teachers and professors expect of them?**[50]
>
> Be a self-starter.
> No excuses—even if they have a legitimate excuse.

encourage them to summarize what they have read. If youth get in the habit of reading to teach a friend or classmate they will do better.[51]

What should they be doing?

There is always a goal that a student needs to be focused upon so help your youth to ask about, "What should I be doing at this point in my life?" For example, high school students should think about the best time to take the SAT or ACT. I recommend they take these exams for the first time no later than the fall semester of their junior year. It is a good idea to take these exams even if the youth is unsure about going to college. Often, it takes time to become familiar with standardized tests, and it helps if the student has three opportunities to take the exam.

I usually suggest that students take the ACT and SAT. Students who tend to be better at taking tests, usually do better on the SAT. Students who struggle with test anxiety but make good grades often do better on the ACT. Engaging in the process in the Junior and Senior year often helps a student become focused on college.

For students who attend college, discourage them from just marking time, and to always think about what the key task for them is at a particular point in time and be looking at the next step to take. Donna Hembrick, the Director of Career Services at North Carolina Central University has identified some key tasks that students need to be accomplishing at particular stages of their training. During their freshmen year they should invest in an interview suit or two, which will be needed later for job interviews and important functions. They should consider doing a summer internship and getting involved in volunteer work. It is also a good idea to get involved in campus organizations that allow them the opportunity to develop leadership skills.

During their sophomore year research at least 3 career options related to their major while pursuing leadership positions in campus organizations. They should ask employers and professors to be prepared to write recommendations to future employers and graduate schools, and make good grades!

Finding graduate schools:
www.Petersons.com

Look carefully then how you walk, not as unwise but as wise, making the best use of the time, because the days are evil. Therefore do not be foolish, but understand what the will of the Lord is.
Ephesians 5:15-17

During their junior year, they need to narrow down their career interests, and start developing their resume and cover letter. If graduate school or professional school is in their future, they should plan to take the Graduate Record Examinations (GRE), Law School Admission Test (LSAT), or Medical College Admission (MCAT) their junior year. They need to get some preparation materials and allow enough time to take these exams more than once so they can obtain the scores they need.

Check out the latest copy of R. N. Bolles' *What Color is Your Parachute?* Published by Ten Speed Press.

During their senior year they need to participate in on-campus recruiting programs, and attend local association meetings and network with potential employers. They should engage in mock interviews for employment positions and graduate school.[52]

Into the Workforce

> *Bondservants, obey in everything those who are*
> *your earthly masters, not by way of eye-service, as*
> *people-pleasers, but with sincerity of heart, fearing*
> *the Lord. Whatever you do, <u>work heartily, as for the</u>*
> *<u>Lord</u> and not for men, knowing that from the Lord*
> *you will receive the inheritance as your reward. You*
> *are serving the Lord Christ. For the wrongdoer will*
> *be paid back for the wrong he has done,*
> *and there is no partiality.*
> *Colossians 3:22-25*

As our youth go into the workforce they can set themselves apart by doing well. According to *State of the American Workplace*, a new report by Gallup Inc., only 30 percent of the U.S. workforce is engaged in their work. The remaining 70 percent of American workers are non-engaged or actively disengaged. This takes a toll and is believed to cost between $450 billion and $550 billion a year to U.S. companies.[53] Unfortunately, meaningful work is not the norm. But if our youth are doing what they love to do and working as if they are doing it for the Lord they will excel. I suspect if you went back to the time of Daniel and picked up an article called *Babylonian Workplace* you would have learned that only 30 percent of the Babylonian workforce was engaged in their work. The remaining 70 percent were non-engaged or actively disengaged at a great cost to the Babylonian kingdom. Daniel, Hananiah, Mishael, and Azariah were engaged and they excelled because they realized God had prepared them for the tasks they were called upon to perform in Babylon. This led them to be engaged in their work and influence their culture. Our youth too can be a influence if they become what God made them to be.

Land the Helicopter

We can expect our youth to struggle with all kinds of adjustments. For example, there is a lot to adjust to when a young person heads to college. In one study, 54 percent of new students reported feeling isolated and lonely; 51 percent reported struggling with absence from family, and 45 percent reported struggling with absence from friends back home.

It is only natural for our youth to initially struggle with these kinds of feelings. If they persist, encourage your youth to utilize their college counseling center. These professionals can help them with these issues and others that may arise.

Other problems may be living situations in the dorm. Encourage them to be proactive about dealing with these issues, not letting them grow into a major difficulty. They key for them is to always try to deal with a situation calmly and objectively.[54]

Resist the temptation to become "helicopter parents." These are parents that become very involved in the lives of their youth and try to micromanage their lives. These youth tend to struggle to learn how to handle situations and may even experience depression as a result. So model, teach, and create, but give them some space to live.

Bring it All Together

Model

You can help your youth by modeling the use of your own interest and personality in your work and hobbies. Be a good steward of what God has given you, and show your youth how they can do the same.

Teach

Constantly teach youth that they are fearfully and wonderfully made. Make it clear they are special, and that God has special tasks for them to perform. Help them see the connection between their interests, aptitude, and personality, and what God is calling them to do.

Create

Create an environment where finding one's skills and identifying how to excel is a priority. Also, have an environment where learning is taking place in some way all of the time.

Chapter 4

Are They
An Investor?

Into the Community

*Build houses and live in them; plant gardens and
eat their produce. Take wives and have sons and
daughters; take wives for your sons, and give your
daughters in marriage, that they may bear sons and
daughters; multiply there, and do not decrease. But
seek the welfare of the city where I have sent you
into exile, and pray to the Lord on its behalf, for in its
welfare you will find your welfare.*
Jeremiah 29:5-7

Jeremiah instructed Judah to build homes, families, and relationships when they were exiled. Though our youth may not be a prisoner in another land, they can learn from the model. To influence the community they must go into it and build relationships. This will require an investment into people.

Daniel was an investor in people. When God gave him the answer to Nebuchadnezzar's dream, Nebuchadnezzar promoted Daniel. Daniel did not forget his friends. Daniel used his position to bring Hananiah, Mishael, and Azariah along with him. Daniel 2:9 says, "<u>Daniel made a request of the king</u>, and he appointed Shadrach, Meshach, and Abednego over the affairs of the province of Babylon. But Daniel remained at the king's court."

Barnabas: A Model Investor in Others

Encourager
Thus Joseph, who was also called by the apostles <u>Barnabas (which means son of encouragement)</u>, a Levite, a native of Cyprus, sold a field that belonged to him and brought the money and laid it at the apostles' feet.
Acts 4:36-37

Connector
And when he had come to Jerusalem, he attempted to join the disciples. And they were all afraid of him, for they did not believe that he was a disciple. But <u>Barnabas took him and brought him to the apostles</u> and declared to them how on the road he had seen the Lord, who spoke to him, and how at Damascus he had preached boldly in the name of Jesus.
Acts 9:26-27

Elevator
While they were worshiping the Lord and fasting, the Holy Spirit said, "Set apart for me <u>Barnabas and Saul</u> for the work to which I have called them."
Acts 13:2

And after the meeting of the synagogue broke up, many Jews and devout converts to Judaism followed <u>Paul and Barnabas,</u> who, as they spoke with them, urged them to continue in the grace of God.
Acts 13:43

We see another example of a man who invested in others in the New Testament when we read about a man named Barnabas. We meet Barnabas in Acts 4:36-37 as he is giving a sizable contribution to the early church. His name had been changed from Joseph to Barnabas which meant encouragement. He must have had a knack for lifting others up. Next we find him ministering to Saul in Acts 9:26-27 who would later become known as Paul. Saul had become a Christian but most of the Christians were afraid of him. Barnabas courageously took Paul and brought him to the apostles. Barnabas saw someone who had potential when he looked at Paul. He nurtured and mentored Paul as our youth may a new student or employee one day. In Acts 11:25, we see that Barnabas went to Tarsus to find Paul and bring him to Antioch where they taught together and took famine relief funds to Judea (Acts 11:30). Barnabas spent time with Paul, and he as well as the entire church benefited from it.

A Risky Investment

And a young man followed him, with nothing but a linen cloth about his body. And they seized him, but he left the linen cloth and ran away naked.
Mark 14:51-52

Now Paul and his companions set sail from Paphos and came to Perga in Pamphylia. And John left them and returned to Jerusalem.
Acts 13:13

That reaped dividends

Aristarchus my fellow prisoner greets you, and Mark the cousin of Barnabas (concerning whom you have received instructions—if he comes to you, welcome him).
Colossians 4:10

Luke alone is with me. Get Mark and bring him with you, for he is very useful to me for ministry.
2 Timothy 4:11

She who is at Babylon, who is likewise chosen, sends you greetings, and so does Mark, my son.
1 Peter 5:13

Often we fail to invest in others because of jealousy, fear of getting proper credit or concern that the one we are helping may surpass us. Barnabas was more concerned about advancing the kingdom than himself. In Acts 13, we see a shift in importance when the names of Paul and Barnabas are reversed. By Acts 14 Paul is being referred to as the chief speaker and appears to be more important than Barnabas.

Rather than becoming jealous, Barnabas was probably thrilled to see God working through him to develop Paul into a great leader. Later Barnabas made a risky investment in a young man named John Mark. Who was John Mark? In the Gospel of Mark we learn that there was a man who was following Jesus as He was about to be crucified. After some young men tried to grab him he ran away naked (Mark 14:51-52). Since Mark's gospel is the only gospel to mention this incident, many conclude the young man was Mark. If this were the case, he probably had a lot to overcome and many questioned the wisdom of Barnabas and Paul in taking him on a grueling missionary journey. The book of Acts indicates that John Mark abandoned the missionary journey (Acts 15:38), which probably led many people to say to Barnabas and Paul, "I told you so." However, when Paul suggested that he and Barnabas return on a missionary journey, trouble arose as Barnabas suggested they take John Mark with them. In Acts 15, we read this lead to a great conflict between Barnabas and Paul and they eventually separated with Paul taking Silas and Barnabas took John Mark on a separate journey. This had to be difficult for Barnabas as his relationship with Paul was strained. Yet Barnabas' investment in John Mark paid dividends.

Ten years later Paul described John Mark as profitable, a fellow worker, and someone he would like to see (Colossians 4:10, Philemon 24; 2 Timothy 4:11). Others also saw the value of John Mark. Peter refered to John Mark as his son (1 Peter 5:13). John Mark wrote the gospel of Mark, which many have characterized as the memoirs of Peter. He is believed to have visited Egypt and founded the church at Alexandria. Many believe as recorded in *Fox's Book of Martyrs* that he was dragged through the streets of Alexandria and killed before their idol, Serapis. John Mark became a man who would not run away or quit even when his life was threatened.

Investing in Others Is an Investment in Themselves

Investing in others is about being in relationship with other people. Relationships are out of vogue these days. Research indicates that people have fewer friends and acquaintances than in the past.[55] Yet, we need friends. Somewhere, either in Judah before the collapse of their country, perhaps on the road to Babylon or after arriving in Babylon, Daniel, Hananiah, Mishael, and Azariah found each other. This helped them to become influencers of the culture rather than being influenced by it. We know from research that people become wise when they associate with wise people and foolish when they associate with foolish people. In a recent study, high school students were asked to categorize their peers as best friends, friends, acquaintances, strangers, or relatives. The researchers then mapped out how students performed in school relative to their peer group. The results indicated that students who associated with other students who performed well academically were themselves more likely to perform well academically. If their grades improved their friends grades improved. The opposite was also true. When a student's GPA dropped, the GPAs of their peers dropped as well.[56] We become like the people we associate with so choose your associates carefully.

I love reading and watching *The Lord of the Rings* by J.R.R. Tolkien, and *The Chronicles of Narnia* by C. S. Lewis. It seems obvious these men had an influence upon one another. For many years C. S. Lewis, J. R. R. Tolkien, Charles Williams, and their friends spent time with one another. Their group of friends became known as "The Inklings." Based on a perusal of the bookshelves of my local bookstore (and a review of top movies over the past years) it appears they continue to influence the culture today. Does this kind of thing happen to people like us?

At Welch College (formerly Free Will Baptist Bible College) a quartet called the Gospeliers formed around the Fall of 1950. At some point, the quartet consisted of Robert Picirilli, Bobby Jackson, James Earl Raper, and Eugene Waddell. They travelled for the college to recruit students and raise funds as they went through school. They continued to do so even after graduating. All four went on to graduate school in South Carolina colleges while continuing to travel for Welch College. They went on to become very successful ministers. Picirilli earned a Ph.D. and returned to Welch College as a professor, and eventually became the Academic Dean. He also served as the moderator of the National Association of Free Will Baptists. Bobby Jackson became the most well-known and traveled evangelist of the Free Will Baptist denomination, and he too served as the moderator of the National Association of Free Will Baptists. James Earl Raper pastored for decades and served as a trustee for Welch College, and headed a children's home in east Tennessee. Eugene Waddell became a pastor and later the director of Free Will Baptist International Missions. Do you think they had an impact upon one another?

Among these were Daniel, Hananiah, Mishael, and
Azariah of the tribe of Judah.
Daniel 1:6

I suspect if you think about your own life you will find evidence of this principle. If you had approached me during my senior year of high school and asked me to name my best friends, I suspect I would have said, "Ronald Suggs and Jerry Jarman." Interestingly, all three of us went on to earn doctorate degrees of some kind. At a recent reunion, I learned that most of our classmates have gone on and become involved in a local church. Proverbs 13:20 teaches us that "Whoever walks with the wise becomes wise, but the companion of fools will suffer harm." I can certainly say that has been true in my life. If our youth are to become wise, they must be around wise people.

Daniel, Hananiah, Mishael, and Azariah were companions. The book of 2 Kings tells us thousands of people were exiled from Judah so there were many others with which they could have associated. What made them decide to build relationships with one another?

*"Daniel, who is <u>one of the exiles from Judah,</u> pays
no attention to you, O king..."*
Daniel 6:13

What should they look for in friends?

*...they sought Daniel and his companions, to kill
them....Then Daniel went to his house and made the
matter known to Hananiah, Mishael, and Azariah,
his companions, and told them to seek mercy from
the God of heaven concerning this mystery, so that
Daniel and his companions might not be destroyed
with the rest of the wise men of Babylon.*
Daniel 2:13, 17-18

Look for Exiles

Arioch referred to Daniel as an exile (Daniel 2:25). Even after experiencing great success, the wicked King Belshazzar called Daniel an exile (Daniel 5:13). When the jealous officials tried to entrap Daniel, they referred to him as an exile (Daniel 6:13). Though Daniel, Hananiah, Mishael, and Azariah had great aptitude, and became very successful the Babylonians always thought of them differently. An exile is someone who is out of place. They do not quite fit in because their home is elsewhere. The writer of Hebrews refers to all believers as exiles.

Encourage your youth to look for people who are more interested in doing what is right than fitting in. There will always be those who adopt the ways of the corrupt culture as a means to fit in, an exile like these four is comfortable being an outsider. They also love the Lord more than the world. To be an exile is to be in good company. Moses became an exile when he chose God over the riches of Egypt.

> ### Exiles
>
> "I have found among the **exiles** from Judah…"
> Daniel 2:25
>
> "…You are that Daniel, one of the **exiles of Judah**, whom the
> king my father brought from Judah."
> Daniel 5:13
>
> …Moses fled and became an **exile**….
> Acts 7:29
>
> These all died in faith…and having acknowledged
> that they were strangers and **exiles on the earth**.
> Hebrews 11:13

In addition to seeking exiles, it is important for our youth to seek those who will help them develop into the people God has planned for them to be.

> ### How does one find a community of "exiles?"
> ### Ask...
>
> Are they comfortable in their own skin?
>
> Is God or other things their top priority?
>
> Do not love the world or the things in the world. If anyone
> loves the world, the love of the Father is not in him.
> 1 John 2:15

Competent to stand in the king's palace,
and to teach them the literature and
language of the Chaldeans.
Daniel 1:4b

Look for Learners

Daniel, Hananiah, Mishael, and Azariah had a desire to learn. Encourage your youth to find places and associate with people where learning is valued, and avoid those who model (and teach) that which is wrong, or are satisfied with mediocrity.

> *Give instruction to a wise man, and he will*
> *be still wiser; teach a righteous man,*
> *and he will increase in learning.*
> *Proverbs 9:9*

When I was in college, I worked at a luxury condominium to help pay my way through school. The residents encouraged us to learn by providing us with newspapers like the Wall Street Journal. In addition, they frequently provided us with educational magazines and books as well as occasional tickets to hear the Nashville Symphony. The workplace seemed to attract people who wanted to learn. Among the group, most went on to earn graduate degrees. The occupations obtained by the workers includes Pastors, University Professors, a College President, an Air Force Chaplain, school teachers, and a publishing company Vice President. Frequent topics for discussion among the workers were how to get into a good graduate school, as well as discussions about music, history, and current events. Though we were from different backgrounds and regions of the country, we all wanted to learn. I learned that in this type of community, competence and a love for learning become contagious.

> *Then <u>Daniel replied with prudence</u> and discretion*
> *to Arioch, the captain of the king's guard, who had*
> *gone out to kill the wise men of Babylon.*
> *Daniel 2:14*

Look for Prudence

> **Characteristics of the Prudent**
>
> In everything _the prudent acts with knowledge_.
> Proverbs 13:16a
>
> One who is wise is _cautious_ and turns away from evil.
> Proverbs 14:16a
>
> The _prudent_ sees danger and hides himself.
> Proverbs 22:3a
>
> It is an honor for a man to keep aloof from strife.
> Proverbs 20:3a

And over them three high officials, of whom Daniel was one, to whom these satraps should give account, so the king might suffer no loss.
Daniel 6:2

Do your children associate with prudent people? Prudence is the ability to know how to act, to behave mannerly. Daniel was a model in prudence. He demonstrated prudence with the eunuch, Arioch, and Nebuchadnezzar. Encourage your youth to spend time with people who are prudent. It is found among those who do their best to avoid evil. They see when danger is present and a situation needs to be avoided. Prudent people do not waste time arguing over trivial matters.

Look for Diligence

The diligence of Daniel led him to ascend as an administrator. Look for diligent people. Diligence is similar to prudence. Diligent people are those who work hard and are focused on getting things done. Diligent people can be entrusted with a task and you can know it will be done. In a community of diligent people there tends to be an atmosphere where work and achievement are the expectation.

> **Characteristics of the Diligent**
>
> The hand of the <u>diligent</u> makes rich.
> He who gathers in summer is a
> prudent son.
> Proverbs 10:4b, 5a
>
> In all toil there is profit.
> Proverbs 14:23a
>
> Whoever works his land will have
> plenty of bread.
> Proverbs 12:11a

Our culture is drifting away from diligence. Today 1 in 7 people between the ages of 16 and 24 in the top 25 major cities U. S. are not in school or working. Diligent people are increasingly in the minority. However, the diligent are likely to grow in popularity just as Daniel, Hananiah, Mishael, and Azariah did. It is estimated that those 1 out of 7 people (5.8 million youth) cost $93.7 billion dollars in government support and in lost revenue every year.[57]

And the king spoke with them, and among all of them none was found like Daniel, Hananiah, Mishael, and Azariah. Therefore they stood before the king.
Daniel 1:19

How do they find them? Thin Slicing

Teach your youth to conduct thin slicing. Thin slicing is the ability to make a quick determination based on a brief interaction. If you think about it, you can identify pretty quickly those who are good for you. Encourage youth to watch what people do, and pay more attention to what they do rather than what they say.

For example, college students are very skilled at thin slicing. Most students can watch a short video of a professor and correctly predict if that professor is effective. Students ratings after viewing a short video of a professor teaching have been found to match the student ratings of instruction the professor receives from students who spend an entire semester with him or her.[58] Physicians can easily look at the vital signs of a patient and quickly determine if their life is in danger. I experienced thin slicing (and have since utilized it) when interviewing for graduate schools.

Thin Slicing by...	Method	Looking for...
Nebuchadnezzar	Questioning	Competence
Abraham's servant	Observation	Care for Others
Jethro	Inquiry	Courage

When she had finished giving him a drink, she said, "I will draw water for your camels also, until they have finished drinking." So she quickly emptied her jar into the trough and ran again to the well to draw water, and she drew for all his camels. _The man gazed at her in silence to learn whether the Lord had prospered his journey or not._
Genesis 24:19-21

They said, "_An Egyptian delivered us out of the hand of the shepherds and even drew water for us and watered the flock._" He said to his daughters, "Then where is he? Why have you left the man? Call him, that he may eat bread."
Exodus 2:19-20

Nebuchadnezzar used thin slicing when he interviewed Daniel, Hananiah, Mishael, and Azariah by the kinds of questions he asked, he was able to determine they were ten times better than the other youth. Abraham's servant used thin slicing to find a wife for Isaac. He prayed that the one who gave him water would be the one (Genesis 24). Moses' father-in-law used thin slicing (before he was Moses' father-in-law) to get Moses into the family. His daughters told him a man had defended them when they were trying to get water for their flock (Exodus 2:19-20). Jethro's response was, "And where is he? Which meant, "Get him; we can use a man like that around here." Some employers use thin slicing when they take an applicant out for dinner and watch how they treat wait staff. Get into the habit of studying people by utilizing thin slicing. Help them watch how people they interact with treat someone they have power and/or position over, perhaps doubting the person can do anything for them.

Proverbs on Those to Avoid	
Characteristic	**Proverb**
The unprepared	A <u>slack</u> hand causes poverty...He who <u>sleeps in harvest</u> is a son who brings <u>shame</u>. Proverbs 10:4a, 5b
The undependable	Like vinegar to the teeth and smoke to the eyes, so is the <u>sluggard</u> to those who send him. Proverbs 10:26
The excuse maker	The sluggard says, "<u>There is a lion outside</u>! I shall be killed in the streets!" Proverbs 22:13
The time waster	He who follows worthless pursuits lacks sense. Proverbs 12:11b
Those who engage in dangerous behavior	The prudent sees danger and hides himself, but <u>the simple go on and suffer for it</u>. Proverbs 22:3
The Talker	Mere talk tends only to poverty. Proverbs 14:23b
The Opinionated	A fool takes no pleasure in understanding, but only in expressing his opinion. Proverbs 18:2

If someone has negative characteristics like those described in the Proverbs, get your youth to ask themselves, "Who is influencing whom?" "Am I becoming more like them or am I influencing them away from these traits?" To influence the culture, they must quickly determine who can help them grow, who they can help grow, and who they should avoid lest they derail them from growing.

Let each of you look not only to his own interests,
but also to the interests of others.
Philippians 2:4

Givers, Takers, and Matchers

Dr. Adam Grant is an Organizational Psychologist who has extensively studied workplace behavior trying to determine who succeeds and who fails. In his book, *Give and Take*, he describes three categories of workers: givers, takers, and matchers. Givers are those who enjoy helping others and will do so with no strings attached, like the Philippians 2 admonition to put the needs of others before yourself. Takers are those who are trying to get as much as they can from people while only giving back what they must. Matchers try to maintain an even balance of give and take. After examining Dr. Grant's research, it appears that his definition of a giver is consistent with the kind of person we are admonished to be in the Scripture. For example, the Good Samaritan is a model for this kind of giving. It also seems consistent with the approach Daniel took as he dealt with others. When Daniel was promoted after finding the answer to King Nebuchadnezzar's dream, he also requested that Hananiah, Mishael, and Azariah be promoted.

Daniel made a request of the king,
and he appointed Shadrach, Meshach,
and Abednego over the affairs of the province of
Babylon. But Daniel remained at the king's court.
Daniel 2:49

We can also see Daniel's behavior as a giver when we look at his work with Nebuchadnezzar and Belshazzar. He tried to help Nebuchadnezzar just before he lost his mind for a period of years, and Belshazzar just before he was overthrown and killed. We are called to give in Scripture, you might say it is a key to the "good life." You would think givers would succeed. When you look at the data, givers sink to the bottom of the success ladder whether you are looking at engineers, salespeople, or physicians. However, givers are also at that top of the success ladder. In the occupations Grant has examined, givers have been at the bottom and the top of the success ladder. How can this be explained? Grant calls the unsuccessful givers selfless givers. They give to others, drop their goals, and give without thinking of the impact. Successful givers are careful to examine who they will help and how much they will help them. Successful givers tend to help other givers or matchers rather than takers. The research indicates it is dangerous to help takers because they will take advantage of you.[59] At first I was bothered by this until I began to realize this is consistent with Scripture.

> *In all things I have shown you that by working hard*
> *in this way we must help the weak and remember the*
> *words of the Lord Jesus, how he himself said, "It is*
> *more blessed to give than to receive."*
> Acts 20:35

Give to Givers

Jesus did not blindly invest in everyone, and neither should our youth. As we examine Jesus' life we see much of it was concentrated on 12 rather than 24 or 36 people. Eleven of the 12 appear to have been givers as exhibited in their selfless sharing of the gospel as seen in Acts 2. Jesus invested in people who were (or became) givers, He instructed us to move to another when our giving is not received. He said in Matthew 10:14, "And if anyone will not receive you or listen to your words, shake off the dust from your feet when you leave that house or town."

Faithful are the wounds of a friend;
profuse are the kisses of an enemy.
Proverbs 27:6

Proverbs 27:17 tells us that as "Iron sharpens iron, one man sharpens another" indicating there can be some friction as we help one another develop. Sometimes development will involve reproof ("Reprove a wise man, and he will love you"—Proverbs 9:8b), letting someone know when they've done something wrong or when there is a better way of doing things. Therefore, the giving and receiving of reproof will be a key element for our youth to help determine if they should continue to give of themselves to a particular person. How do they know if they are dealing with a taker? Throughout Proverbs there are three types of problematic people that are mentioned: the simple, scoffers, and fools.

How long, O <u>simple</u> ones, will you love being sim-
ple? How long will <u>scoffers</u> delight in their
scoffing and <u>fools</u> hate knowledge?
Proverbs 1:22

Avoid Scoffers
The Proverbs teach us to avoid the scoffer. What is a scoffer? The scoffer is a person who hates truth and ridicules those who try to correct them. Scoffers are often cynical and bitter. Our youth run the risk of being influenced by them if they remain with scoffers, which is one reason we are told to avoid them. How do our youth know they can

not help them? Encourage them to consider Jesus' model for confrontation in Matthew 18, when dealing with the scoffer. There comes a time when it is obvious a person will not listen to them and at that point, it becomes an issue of being a good steward of the amount of time they have. So our youth should avoid the scoffer so the scoffer cannot influence them, and so they may invest their time in more productive efforts. Also, isolating the scoffer might actually give them the opportunity to see their error and cease scoffing.

How do they know?	
Hatred for correction	But he who hates reproof is stupid. Proverbs 12:1b
	A scoffer does not like to be reproved; he will not go to the wise. Proverbs 15:12
Attacks helper	Whoever corrects a scoffer gets himself abuse, and he who reproves a wicked man incurs injury. Do not reprove a scoffer, or he will hate you. Proverbs 9:7-8a

Avoid Fools

A second group of people we are told to avoid are fools. The foolish are dangerous. They do things that waste time, and inflict harm. They drag people down and can do much damage. Our youth can try to help them with correction as we are instructed to provide in Proverbs 26:5, "Answer a fool according to his folly, lest he be wise in his own eyes."

If they respond, our youth can be a positive influence in their life. If the fool fails to respond positively it will become time to move on as Proverbs 26:4 indicates, "Answer not a fool according to his folly, lest you be like him yourself."

How do you know?

Despise instruction	*Fools despise wisdom and instruction. Proverbs 1:7b*
Proud of being stupid	*In everything the prudent acts with knowledge, but a fool flaunts his folly. Proverbs 13:16*
Bad influence	*Leave the presence of a fool, for there you do not meet words of knowledge. Proverbs 14:7*
Dangerous	*Whoever ignores instruction despises himself. Proverbs 15:32a*
	Let a man meet a she-bear robbed of her cubs rather than a fool in his folly. Proverbs 17:12
	A fool is reckless and careless. Proverbs 14:16b

There is a clear difference between those we are to avoid and those we are called upon to embrace.

Proverbs on Those to Embrace

Trait	Proverb
Careful	*The prudent gives thought to his steps. Proverbs 14:15b*
Confidant	*A man of understanding remains silent. Proverbs 11:12b*
Truth teller	*Righteous lips are the delight of a king, and he loves him who speaks what is right. Proverbs 16:13*
Humble	*Humility comes before honor. Proverbs 15:33b*
Generous	*He who is generous to the needy honors him. Proverbs 14:31b*

Build Relationships

In 1985, the typical person had three people with whom they could confide important information. Twenty years later in 2004, the typical person indicated they had zero people with whom they could confide. This is very sad.[60] A researcher challenged these findings which led to a reexamination of the data. The results supported the earlier findings and further indicated a gap in relationships is often concealed by the prevalence of social networks. In other words, people have fewer and fewer friends today, though often this problem is concealed by a larger number of friends on Facebook or followers on Twitter. In fact, the number of close friends and confidants has actually decreased since the arrival of social media.[61] Truly, our youth will be an outlier should they engage in building relationships.

Be Friendly

A man that hath friends must shew himself friendly:
and there is a friend that sticketh closer than a brother.
Proverbs 18:24 KJV

To begin to build relationships they must be intentional about being friendly and spending quality time with those they target. They can start by really being with people. This means there will be times when they put the cell phone and other media aside. We know from research that the mere presence of a cell phone on a table reduces in-person conversation quality. In one study, researchers placed a mobile phone of the participants on a table between them. They were compared to a group who placed a spiral notebook between them and a peer. The results indicated that the presence of the cell phone negatively affected closeness, connection, and conversation quality.[62] To be friendly, our youth need to be with whomever they are with rather than being focused on texting or other media.

Be Kind

Encourage youth to bear with others realizing they aren't perfect, and to be willing to give them the benefit of doubt. We want them to go out of their way to be kind to others and forgive them of their imperfections. It also helps to put Ephesians 4:32 into practice, "Be kind to one another, tenderhearted, forgiving one another, as God in Christ forgave you."

Be a Confidant

It helps if they establish themselves as trustworthy, Proverbs 11:13 says, "He who is <u>trustworthy</u> in spirit keeps a thing covered." They must be capable of being entrusted to maintain the confidence of others. They should not repeat what other people tell them. They need to be alert for the gossip kings and queens who fish for information about others, and develop a habit of talking to people rather than about other people.

Be There

> Two are better than one, because they have a good reward for their toil. For if they fall, one will lift up his fellow. But woe to him who is alone when he falls and has not another to lift him up! Again, if two lie together, they keep warm, but how can one keep warm alone? And though a man might prevail against one who is alone, two will withstand him—a threefold cord is not quickly broken.
> Ecclesiastes 4:9-12

Proverbs 17:17 says, "A friend loves at all times, and a brother is born for adversity."

Teach youth to model the warm relationship described in Ecclesiastes 4:11 with others. Also, train youth to be there for their friend as they encounter difficulty. Real relationships are built when our youth help their friends in time of need. When friends encounter difficulties, be they school or work problems, relationship problems, or health problems encourage our youth to be there for their friends. The opposite is also true. When our youth encounter difficulties, they need to note those who are around them at that time. They are the real friends who will help our youth survive and thrive.

Be a Mentor

Encourage your youth to invest in someone by finding those who are not as far along as they are. Perhaps they are younger or new to a place where our youth are. A good model for this kind of investment is what Barnabas gave to Paul after he became a believer.

What is mentoring?

Characteristic	Titus 2
A willingness to be different	1 But as for you, teach what accords with sound doctrine.
Showing people how to live	2 Older men are to be sober-minded, dignified, self-controlled, sound in faith, in love, and in steadfastness. 3 Older women likewise are to be reverent in behavior, not slanderers or slaves to much wine. They are to teach what is good,... 7 Show yourself in all respects to be a model of good works, and in your teaching show integrity, dignity, 8 and sound speech that cannot be condemned,
Training	4 and so train...5 to be self-controlled, pure, working...6 Likewise, urge the younger men to be self-controlled.
Practical	9...be submissive to their own masters in everything; they are to be well-pleasing, not argumentative, 10 not pilfering, but showing all good faith, so that in everything they may adorn the doctrine of God our Savior. 12 training us to renounce ungodliness and worldly passions, and to live self-controlled, upright, and godly lives in the present age,...15 Declare these things; exhort and rebuke with all authority. Let no one disregard you.
Why mentor?	5...that the word of God may not be reviled. 8...so that an opponent may be put to shame, having nothing evil to say about us.

Find a Mentor

Our youth will also need to find mentors wherever they are. They can look for them among their pastors, teachers, professors, supervisors, older students, and more experienced employees. A good place to find mentors is in a local church.

Find a Church

Make it clear to your youth, wherever they go, they will always need to be part of a family of believers. The Bible teaches us that a Christian without a church community is vulnerable. God uses the church to impact the world so they need to find a church and get involved. Encourage them to resist the temptation to church shop or become a critic of churches. Help them find a body of believers, when they go off to college or move away and unite with

> **Pray We**
>
> *Then I turned my face to the Lord God, seeking him by prayer and pleas for mercy with fasting and sackcloth and ashes.*
> *Daniel 9:3*
>
> *I prayed to the LORD my God and <u>made confession</u>, saying, "O Lord, the great and awesome God, who keeps covenant and steadfast love with those who love him and keep his commandments, <u>we have sinned</u> and done wrong and acted wickedly and rebelled, turning aside from your commandments and rules.*
> *Daniel 9:4-5*
>
> *<u>We</u> have not listened to your servants the prophets, who spoke in your name to our kings, our princes, and our fathers, and to all the people of the land.*
> *Daniel 9:6*

them in spite of their imperfections and immerse themselves into the body. Note, there are no perfect churches so discourage them from running at the first sign of difficulty. Someone has described a church as a group of porcupines on a winter night. They seriously need to get close to one another for warmth but are constantly pricking one another. Today the tendency is for one to become upset with people at a church and then move on to the next one. If our youth run at the first sign of trouble they will be robbed of their ability to mature and develop. Encourage them to get in the habit of seeing themselves as part of the church and responsible for its success. Note the way Daniel saw himself and prayed for the people of Judah (Daniel 9). Had Daniel committed egregious sins? Probably not—but he constantly prayed "I" and "we." He identified with Judah and accepted responsibility for their action. He considered himself a participant rather than a spectator.

What should our youth look for in a church community? Help them look for a place where they will be challenged to grow in the Word, and look for people who will be good models for learning how to live. They should also look for a place to get involved and use their gifts, and remember there are no perfect churches.

When I was in college I had a privilege of playing (mostly I just practiced with the team) on the first basketball team at Welch College. Previously most of us had been on various society sports teams where we competed against each other. To address some of this our coach implemented an exercise where we would end practice every morning with a teammate shooting free throws. If the teammate made both free throws, practice was over. But if they missed, we had to run what was called suicides (a well named exercise). We then returned to the baseline and another teammate would shoot again. If they missed, we ran again. As a result, this group of rivals quickly meshed into what became a real team. It did not matter who was at the free throw line, it felt like we all were there. Encourage your youth to choose their community carefully but once they choose, think and pray "we." Stick it out in the good times as well as the bad and they along with the community will grow.

Interaction in the Church

How should they interact with others at the church? According to Titus 2, it is wise to find older people in their church and to get to know them. It can be hard to interact with people from another generation, but the Scripture will help. We are told in 1 Timothy 5:1, "Do not rebuke an older man." Rebuking an older man can be a real relationship killer! The passage goes on to say instead "encourage him as you would a father." So train youth to treat older people as they would like people to treat their parents or grandparents. Also encourage your youth to try to seek out the older people in their church and minister to them by visiting with them. Tell them to ask questions about their life, and take advantage of these opportunities. Remember, they are helping themselves as well as the person they are with.

Get to know an older couple at your church
Questions to ask:

How did you meet your spouse?

What was it like when you were growing up?

What advice do you have for me as I grow?

The Scripture also teaches us how to treat same age peers as siblings (1 Timothy 5:2). You are probably recognizing a theme, the community of the church is a family where we help one another as we walk with the Lord.

"Behold, the days are coming, when all that is in your house, and that which your fathers have stored up till this day, shall be carried to Babylon. Nothing shall be left, says the LORD. And some of your own sons, who will come from you, whom you will father, shall be taken away, and they shall be eunuchs in the palace of the king of Babylon."
Isaiah 39:6-7

To Marry or Not to Marry

*Now as a concession, not a command,
I say this. I wish that all were as I myself am.*

But each has his own gift from God,
one of one kind and one of another.
1 Corinthians 7:6-7

As you read the book of Daniel there is no mention of Daniel, Hananiah, Mishael, or Azariah having a wife. One hundred years before the fall of Jerusalem, King Hezekiah attempted to gain favor from the Babylonians by showing them his treasures. He was being disobedient to God, and he was depending upon the Babylonians to protect him (rather than God) from Assyria. The prophecy in Isaiah 39:7 indicates that many of the royal family will become eunuchs and serve in the palace of the king of Babylon. Therefore, it is very possible that Daniel, Hananiah, Mishael, and Azariah may have been eunuchs. If this were the case, clearly a single person can impact the culture. We see further evidence of this when Paul admonished those who can be single to consider it a gift and a way to serve the Lord unencumbered (1 Corinthians 7:7). Our youth will have to make their own determination about whether God has called them to be single.

Finding a Spouse

An excellent wife who can find?
She is far more precious than jewels.
Proverbs 31:10

Should they choose to be single, they should do so for the right reasons. There is an alarming trend in our culture where many are turned off by the idea of marriage. So if your youth get married, they will be in the minority in the United States.[63] Many are cohabitating, engaging in the sexual hook up culture but are not interested in building a family or being a spouse. After deciding to follow Christ, the most important decision they will make is if they should get married and if so to whom. The same strategies previously described like thin slicing can help them to identify a spouse.

Thin Slicing on What to Avoid

Nonbelievers	*Do not be unequally yoked with unbelievers. For what partnership has righteousness with lawlessness? Or what fellowship has light with darkness? 2 Corinthians 6:14*
Criticism	*But now you must put them all away: anger, wrath, malice, slander, and obscene talk from your mouth. Colossians 3:8*
	Let no corrupting talk come out of your mouths, but only such as is good for building up, as fits the occasion, that it may give grace to those who hear. Ephesians 4:29
Contempt	*But if you bite and devour one another, watch out that you are not consumed by one another. Galatians 5:15*
Defensiveness	*Therefore, confess your sins to one another and pray for one another, that you may be healed. The prayer of a righteous person has great power as it is working. James 5:16*
Stonewalling	*Be angry and do not sin; do not let the sun go down on your anger. Ephesians 4:26*

In fact, Dr. John Gottman, a psychologist with decades of experience has conducted extensive research on marital relationships.

Gottman has been able to look at couples before they are married and predict with 94 percent accuracy who will stay together. He identified four key characteristics that are toxic to the marital relationship: criticism, contempt, stonewalling, and defensiveness.[64] They can use thin slic-

Go beyond looks

*Like a gold ring in a pig's snout is a beautiful woman without discretion.
Proverbs 11:22*

*An excellent wife is the crown of her husband, but she who brings shame is like rottenness in his bones.
Proverbs 12:4*

ing by looking for these characteristics to determine if they are in a healthy relationship. The best predictor of future behavior is past behavior. If they find themselves being treated with contempt or a lot of criticism, they are in an unhealthy relationship. Whatever they see in a dating relationship will likely be magnified many times over should they marry the person.

How can they know what someone is like? Again, look at thin slicing. Abraham's servant knew he had a good prospect in Rebecca when she willingly provided water for him and his camels (Genesis 24). She was caring and industrious. Our youth too must be on the lookout for someone of virtue.

Thin Slicing in Dating

Sacrifices for you	*Husbands, love your wives, as Christ loved the church and gave himself up for her,… In the same way husbands should love their wives as their own bodies. He who loves his wife loves himself. For no one ever hated his own flesh, but nourishes and cherishes it, just as Christ does the church. Ephesians 5:25, 28-29*
Makes you the top priority	*"Therefore a man shall leave his father and mother and hold fast to his wife, and the two shall become one flesh." This mystery is profound, and I am saying that it refers to Christ and the church. However, let each one of you love his wife as himself, and let the wife see that she respects her husband. Ephesians 5:31-33*
Trustworthy	*The heart of her husband trusts in her, and he will have no lack of gain. She does him good, and not harm, all the days of her life. Proverbs 31:11-12*
Will take care of the family	*She seeks wool and flax, and works with willing hands. She is like the ships of the merchant; she brings her food from afar. Proverbs 31:13-14*

Willing to work to provide	*She rises while it is yet night and provides food for her household and portions for her maidens. Proverbs 31:15*
Compassionate	*She opens her hand to the poor and reaches out her hands to the needy. Proverbs 31:20*
Honorable	*Her husband is known in the gates when he sits among the elders of the land. She makes linen garments and sells them; she delivers sashes to the merchant. Strength and dignity are her clothing, and she laughs at the time to come. Proverbs 31:23-25*
Wise and Kind	*She opens her mouth with wisdom, and the teaching of kindness is on her tongue. Proverbs 31:26*

I experienced a bit of this kind of thin slicing when I was in college. We had a tradition where young men would send letters to young ladies each night and the ladies would reciprocate. Keep in mind this was well before the days of cell phones. So it was a big deal for all of us. People would wait around and look forward to the letters each evening. One night I was walking by the library and a young lady told me she bet she could get every girl from the girls dorm to write me. It was a big joke and she tried to make it happen. Later that night it appeared, I had letters from everyone in the girls dorm. As I went through the letters, I noted there was at least one girl who did not send a letter—Lynne Harmon. She sent me a subtle message that night. If you want a letter from me you'll need to write me first. I got the message. Several years later she became my wife.

Bring it Together

Model

Model the importance of relationship by investing your life in those of others. Involve your youth in these activities (e.g., visiting with, having dinner with others). By your actions show them what a real friendship looks like.

Teach

Spend a lot of time discussing the teaching of Proverbs on peer relationships. Help your youth sort out the influence they have upon others, and how others influence them. Teach them the art of thin slicing by helping them analyze their own life situations.

Create

Create an environment where people matter more than things, where there is an outward rather than an inward focus. Create a situation where the norm is to be focused on others rather than gratifying oneself.

Chapter 5

Are They An Influencer?

Invest in the Culture

Build houses and live in them; plant gardens and eat their produce. Take wives and have sons and daughters; take wives for your sons, and give your daughters in marriage, that they may bear sons and daughters; multiply there, and do not decrease. But <u>seek the welfare of the city where I have sent you into exile</u>, and pray to the LORD on its behalf, for in its welfare you will find your welfare.
Jeremiah 29:5-7

Jeremiah told the exiles to seek the welfare of the city where they were sent. Our youth too must seek to help the community wherever they go. If they are prepared, know who they are, and are part of a community of believers, they are ready to go into the culture. Maybe they are in a workplace where they are the only Christian, a secular university where many are antagonistic to their faith, or a missionary in a place where no one knows about Christ. They are in the culture. What do they do?

> *Do all things <u>without grumbling</u> or disputing, that you may be <u>blameless</u> and innocent, children of God without blemish <u>in the midst</u> of a crooked and twisted generation, among whom you <u>shine</u> as lights in the world, <u>holding fast</u> to the word of life...*
> *Philippians 2:14-16a*

Resist the Urge to Complain

Instead of grumbling, encourage them to consider the words of Mordecai to Esther (Esther 4:14) long ago when she found herself in a corrupt culture, "Who knows whether you have not come...for such a time as this?" Also, embrace the admonition of Paul to seek to influence the culture without grumbling. Our youth can have an influence by living blamelessly. It is easy to become bitter about what has happened to our culture but this can lead us to harm others rather than pointing them to God.

Look for Opportunities

Teach them to look for opportunities to be salt and light to those that are around them. Consider how Daniel was ready when Nebuchadnezzar ordered the killing of the wise men. Instead of being consumed with his own concerns, he calmly sought a solution and saved the wise men.

> *Daniel answered the king and said, "No wise men, enchanters, magicians, or astrologers can show to the king the mystery that the king has asked, but there is a God in heaven who reveals mysteries, and*

*he has made known to King Nebuchadnezzar what
will be in the latter days. Your dream and the visions
of your head as you lay in bed are these.*
Daniel 2:27-28

Though his life was in danger, Daniel laid the groundwork by briefly mentioning God when he was brought before King Nebuchadnezzar.

At the conclusion of the interpretation of the dream, Daniel stated...

*"...just as you saw that a stone was cut from a
mountain by no human hand, and that it broke in
pieces the iron, the bronze, the clay, the silver, and
the gold. A great God has made known to the king
what shall be after this. The dream is certain, and its
interpretation sure."*
Daniel 2:45

When our youth receive an opportunity, they need to be clear, concise, and congenial in their presentation of the gospel. Also, encourage them to remember our Sovereign God will present other opportunities and use other people to influence the culture. Later God used Hananiah, Mishael, and Azariah to influence King Nebuchadnezzar during the fiery furnace incident where they briefly witnessed to him.

> ## A Crisis Leads to an Opportunity
>
> The king answered and said to the Chaldeans, "The word from me is firm: if you do not make known to me the dream and its interpretation, you shall be torn limb from limb, and your houses shall be laid in ruins."
> Daniel 2:5
>
> He declared to Arioch, the king's captain, "Why is the decree of the king so urgent?" Then Arioch made the matter known to Daniel. And Daniel went in and requested the king to appoint him a time, that he might show the interpretation to the king.
> Daniel 2:15-16
>
> Therefore Daniel went in to Arioch, whom the king had appointed to destroy the wise men of Babylon. He went and said thus to him: "Do not destroy the wise men of Babylon; bring me in before the king, and I will show the king the interpretation."
> Daniel 2:24

Shadrach, Meshach, and Abednego answered and said to the king, "O Nebuchadnezzar, we have no need to answer you in this matter. If this be so, our God whom we serve is able to deliver us from the burning fiery furnace, and he will deliver us out of your hand, O king. But if not, be it known to you, O king, that we will not serve your gods or worship the golden image that you have set up."
Daniel 3:16-18

Our youth need to be prepared to present a witness on the Bible as the Word of God, the resurrection of Christ, God's plan for the family, and their own reason for hope. They should look forward to these opportunities rather than avoiding them.

*But in your hearts honor Christ the Lord as holy,
always being prepared to make a defense to anyone
who asks you for a reason for the hope that is in
you; yet do it with gentleness and respect.*
1 Peter 3:15

Be a Small Target

In 1 Peter 4:15-16 the Scripture says, "But let none of you suffer as a murderer or a thief or an evildoer or as a meddler. Yet if anyone suffers as a Christian, let him not be ashamed, but let him glorify God in that name." In essence, Peter is telling us to be a small target. If our youth are going to get in trouble, let it be for doing what they should do, instead of what they should not do.

We want our youth to try to be people of integrity so that no one will have a reason to attack them. Hananiah, Mishael, and Azariah did not get into trouble because they were slack at their work. They were attacked because they refused to bow to Nebuchadnezzar's image (Daniel 3:8-12).

When it came time to try to attack Daniel there was nothing that could be used against him except his faith. Daniel 6:5 says, "Then these men said, "We shall not find any ground for complaint against this Daniel unless we find it in connection with the law of his God." Let that be the case for our youth as well. Encourage them not to worry, God will take care of their enemies.

Enemies are Opportunities

In fact, we want our youth to view enemies as opportunities. Before Jesus instructed us in Matthew 5:44 to "love your enemies and pray for those who persecute you," Daniel put that into practicve. Nebuchadnezzar encountered many obstacles. Each time, it appears Daniel did his best to help him. If you had been in Daniel's shoes would you have been willing to help Nebuchadnezzar? Consider the chart below which shows the many reasons Daniel could have been angry with Nebuchadnezzar.

Did Daniel have anything to be angry about?

Mistreatment of his king	*Against him came up Nebuchadnezzar king of Babylon and bound him in chains to take him to Babylon. 2 Chronicles 36:6*
Mistreatment of the weak	*Therefore he brought up against them the king of the Chaldeans, who killed their young men with the sword in the house of their sanctuary and had no compassion on young man or virgin, old man or aged. He gave them all into his hand. 2 Chronicles 36:17*
Destruction of the homeland	*And they burned the house of God and broke down the wall of Jerusalem and burned all its palaces with fire and destroyed all its precious vessels. 2 Chronicles 36:19*
Killing of a king's sons	*Then they captured the king and brought him up to the king of Babylon at Riblah, and they passed sentence on him. They slaughtered the sons of Zedekiah before his eyes, and put out the eyes of Zedekiah and bound him in chains and took him to Babylon. 2 Kings 25:6-7*
Attempted to kill his friends	*Then Nebuchadnezzar was filled with fury, and the expression of his face was changed against Shadrach, Meshach, and Abednego. He ordered the furnace heated seven times more than it was usually heated. And he ordered some of the mighty men of his army to bind Shadrach, Meshach, and Abednego, and to cast them into the burning fiery furnace. Daniel 3:19-20*

For 18 years Judah was oppressed by the Babylonian regime. This oppression culminated with the destruction of Jerusalem and the burning of the temple in 586 B.C. If you were doing a modern day Hollywood movie about the lives of Daniel, Hananiah, Mishael, and Azariah, it would probably involve them seeking revenge for what was done to their homeland.

Daniel clearly had a reason to be angry with Nebuchadnezzar. However, I believe as Dr. Douglas Simpson suggested in his book on Daniel that he prayed for Nebuchadnezzar for some 30 years.[65] Perhaps Daniel's approach began, as Jesus would later command, with praying for an enemy.

> *Then Daniel, whose name was Belteshazzar, was dismayed for a while, and his thoughts alarmed him. The king answered and said, "Belteshazzar, let not the dream or the interpretation alarm you." Belteshazzar answered and said, "My lord, may the dream be for those who hate you and its interpretation for your enemies!"*
> *Daniel 4:19*

When we care for an enemy as Jesus commanded, it truly sets the believer apart from the non-believer. How do we know that Daniel was not filled with hatred toward Nebuchadnezzar? In Daniel 4:19-27, we see Daniel relay the news to Nebuchadnezzar that he would lose his mind. This was the perfect time for Daniel to gloat in the misfortune of this man who had done so much harm to those he loved. Yet Daniel did not gloat. He was dismayed when he realized the trouble that was about to befall the king. Daniel tried to help Nebuchadnezzar.

> *"Therefore, O king, let my counsel be acceptable to you: break off your sins by practicing righteousness, and your iniquities by showing mercy to the oppressed, that there may perhaps be a lengthening of your prosperity."*
> *Daniel 4:27*

Daniel truly cared about Nebuchadnezzar. Our youth must have the same concern for those in their community.

Forgive

Some might say that Daniel had over identified with his captor and that he had tried to suppress what Nebuchadnezzar had truly done to him and Judah. I suggest instead that Daniel had truly forgiven Nebuchadnezzar. I also suspect we can learn from him as well. It is critical that our youth forgive if they are to have physical, spiritual, and psychological health.

Jesus' Solution for Enemies

"You have heard that it was said, 'You shall love your neighbor and hate your enemy.' But I say to you, Love your enemies and pray for those who persecute you, so that you may be sons of your Father who is in heaven. For he makes his sun rise on the evil and on the good, and sends rain on the just and on the unjust. For if you love those who love you, what reward do you have? Do not even the tax collectors do the same?
Matthew 5:43-46

Pray for the Offender

In studies on forgiveness, those in prayer and devotional groups have been found to be more likely to forgive. It appears that when we pray for an offender, we develop empathy for them. Similarly, when we read biblical passages on forgiveness we are more likely to forgive.[66]

Acknowledgement of a Calamity

By bringing upon us a great calamity. For under the whole heaven there has not been done anything like what has been done against Jerusalem. Daniel 9:12b

As it is written in the Law of Moses, all this calamity has come upon us; yet we have not entreated the favor of the LORD our God, turning from our iniquities and gaining insight by your truth. Daniel 9:13

Therefore the LORD has kept ready the calamity and has brought it upon us, for the Lord our God is righteous in all the works that he has done, and we have not obeyed his voice. Daniel 9:14

In his work on forgiveness, Dr. Robert Enright indicated there is a process many appear to go through as they forgive. This includes an acknowledgement of what has been done, gaining perspective upon what has happened; and building positive thoughts and behaviors.[67] Nearly 70 years after the exile began, Daniel prayed about what had happened to Judah. He made it clear that it was a calamity.

However, Daniel also acknowledged that Judah had behaved treacherously thereby providing some perspective for what had transpired. Our youth learn from him by acknowledging when they have been wronged and searching for perspective upon what has happened.

Too often we assume that when someone has been wronged their life has been irreparably damaged and even shortened. That was not the case with Daniel or apparently with other people. For example, an interesting study out of the University of Haifa in Israel examined 55,000 Polish immigrants who came to Israel between 1945 until 1950 and another group that came prior to 1939. The researchers found that the men who had experienced the Holocaust at 10 to 15 years of age lived on average 10 months more than the men who were already in Israel. Youth who were 16 to 20 years of age and experienced the Holocaust lived an extra 18 months longer that those who did not experience the Holocaust. It has been hypothesized that the Holocaust survivors lived longer in spite of the trauma they experienced, because of a renewed sense of purpose and meaning.[68]

From the Scripture, it appears that Daniel understood that Nebuchadnezzar's actions were brought on by the sins of Judah. This probably prevented him from sitting around and thinking about how evil Nebuchadnezzar was and allowed him to move forward and minister to him. Similarly, Joseph acknowledged the evil his brothers perpetrated upon him in Genesis 50. Yet, he appeared to have a perspective for the situation and indicated the event had been used by God to save many people. The lesson for our youth is not to minimize some evil someone has done to them, but to acknowledge it and try to move past it, looking for perspective, how something positive might come out of it and then to move on.

Also, it is not wise to simply dwell on how they have been wronged or a person with whom they have had a difficulty. For example, the research indicates that using Facebook to keep tabs on an ex after a breakup may delay emotional recovery and personal growth. In one study, people who spent the most time on their ex-partner's Facebook page had more distress, negative feelings, and longing for their former flames and lower levels of personal growth.[69] As Proverbs 26:20 says, "For lack of wood the fire goes out, and where there is no whisperer, quarreling ceases."

If your enemy is hungry, give him bread to eat, and if
he is thirsty, give him water to drink.
Proverbs 25:21

Do something good for their enemy

It appears that as a young man Daniel is clearly trying to point Nebuchadnezzar to God when the lives of the wise men were threatened. Before interpreting Nebuchadnezzar's dream, Daniel said, "There is a God in heaven who reveals mysteries, and he has made known to King Nebuchadnezzar what will be in the latter days. Your dream and the visions of your head as you lay in bed are these (Daniel 2:28). Daniel was witnessing to Nebuchadnezzar, trying to show him the truth.

We can learn from Daniel, when our youth do something nice for someone it makes our youth have a more positive view of people. When they harm someone or talk despairingly about people, it leads them to dislike people more. Part of the forgiveness process for Daniel was actually trying to help Nebuchadnezzar find God.

Was it worth it?

It appears Nebuchadnezzar became quite fond of Daniel. When Daniel interpreted Nebuchadnezzar's dream, according to Daniel 2:46, "King Nebuchadnezzar fell upon his face and paid homage to Daniel, and commanded that an offering and incense be offered up to him." Nebuchadnezzar also began to speak favorably of God, "The king answered and said to Daniel, "Truly, your God is God of gods and Lord of kings, and a revealer of mysteries, for you have been able to reveal this mystery." Though Nebuchadnezzar did not immediately become a follower of God, he acknowledged God's supremacy as a god, and he kept Daniel close throughout his reign (Daniel 2:49).

Critics often look at Daniel 3 and ask about the whereabouts of Daniel during the fiery furnace episode. As our youth interact with people in the culture, they will learn that people who have authority over them might not want them around when they are about to make a decision about which they know our youth will disagree. Nebuchadnezzar would have known Daniel well enough to realize he would object to the building of his golden image, and would never bow to such a thing. I also suspect he was fond enough of Daniel (or dependent upon his expertise) that he did not wish to lose him. To deal with this I think that Nebuchadnezzar would have sent Daniel away on business during this time. If this is what transpired it shows that Nebuchadnezzar did not want Daniel around when he did something he ought not to do and it suggests that Daniel was having an impact upon his culture.

In Daniel 2, Nebuchadnezzar praises God but then falters with the building of the fiery furnace in Daniel 3. The next interaction we see between Nebuchadnezzar and Daniel is in Daniel 4. It is important to note that Nebuchadnezzar is doing the talking in this example. Note the similarity between Daniel 4:3 and Psalm 145:13.

How great are his signs, how mighty his wonders!
His kingdom is an everlasting kingdom, and his do-
minion endures from generation to generation.
Daniel 4:3

Your kingdom is an everlasting kingdom, and your
dominion endures throughout all generations.
Psalm 145:13

After King Nebuchadnezzar recounts his experience he appears to acknowledge God as the God.

> "At the end of the days I, Nebuchadnezzar, lifted my eyes to heaven, and my reason returned to me, and I blessed the Most High, and praised and honored him who lives forever, for his dominion is an everlasting dominion, and his kingdom endures from generation to generation; all the inhabitants of the earth are accounted as nothing, and he does according to his will among the host of heaven and among the inhabitants of the earth; and none can stay his hand or say to him, "What have you done?...Now I, Nebuchadnezzar, praise and extol and honor the King of heaven, for all his works are right and his ways are just; and those who walk in pride he is able to humble."
> Daniel 4:34-35, 37

Did Nebuchadnezzar become a believer? I do not know, but one thing is certain. He was definitely influenced by some exiles from Judah.

Don't Quit!

Still at Work

Belshazzar did not appear to have a high regard for Daniel. That did not stop Daniel from faithfully working. It was during Belshazzar's reign that we received those interesting visions.

In the first year of Belshazzar king of Babylon, Daniel saw a dream and visions of his head as he lay in his bed. Then he wrote down the dream and told the sum of the matter.
Daniel 7:1

> *In the third year of the reign of King Belshazzar a vision appeared to me, Daniel, after that which appeared to me at the first.*
> *Daniel 8:1*

It appears that the descendants of Nebuchadnezzar did not value Daniel. But when Belshazzar needed some help with an interpretation, the Queen Mother reminded him of a man "in whom is the spirit of the holy gods." She lists specific character qualities Daniel possessed. Belshazzar sent for Daniel and seems to treat him with disrespect by calling him an exile. This shows that though they may not be valued, if our youth possess competence people will eventually seek out their services.

Daniel was competent enough to serve in whatever administration might be in power. He served at least until 539 B.C. In Daniel 6, a new administration arose and the king saw Daniel's competence and made him one of three governors (Daniel 6:2). Look at verse 3.

> *"Daniel became <u>distinguished</u> above all the other high officials and satraps, because an excellent spririt was in him. And the king planned to set him over the whole kingdom."*
> *Daniel 6:3*

Daniel was likable and that attitude distinguished him. Daniel could do things that needed done. To the point that his enemies could only find one fault in him—he prayed. They attacked his identity as a follower of God. A law was passed making it illegal to pray. Seventy years later Daniel faces another test. How did he respond? Daniel 6:10 (NKJV) says, "Now when Daniel knew that the writing was signed, he went home. And in his upper room, with his windows open toward Jerusalem, he knelt down on his knees three times that day, and prayed and gave thanks before his God, <u>as was his custom since early days</u>."

Where is Daniel Buried?

Would you like to visit the grave of Daniel? You can visit a Tomb of Daniel in Susa, Iran. However, near Mala Amir, in Khuzestan of Iran there are others who claim to have the grave of Daniel. There are tombs for Daniel in Iraq as well (Babylon, Kirkuk, and Muqdadiyah). There is at least one more site that claims to have the tomb of Daniel, that is found in Samarkand, Uzbekistan. Not bad for a fellow who was an exile.

Bring it All Together

Model

In a way, everything in Daniel's life was brought together in this event. The Scripture indicates that he did exactly what he had done his entire life ("since early days"), meaning he had been praying this way since a child.

I have often wondered why Daniel did not just pray as he walked around, or while he was sitting in a chair so no one would know he was praying. Praying as he prayed was part of who he was, his identity, that is why Daniel was able to live with such certainty. He had a real relationship with the Lord. That prayer life defined him, and nothing would interfere with that relationship. I also suspect he may have prayed the way he did because that is what his parents had modeled, hence it was very personal to him.

Teach

First Kings 8:33 and 35 says, "When your people Israel are defeated before the enemy because they have sinned against you, and if they turn again to you and acknowledge your name and pray and plead with you...if they <u>pray toward this place</u> and acknowledge your name and turn from their sin, when you afflict them…" Did Daniel's parents teach him to pray toward Jerusalem? Though we cannot know for sure, I think they did. We do know from the Scripture that he prayed three times that day. That was very likely in obedience to Psalm 55:17, "Evening and morning and at noon I utter my complaint and moan, and he hears my voice."

Create

There were probably many things in the home of Daniel that reminded him of the God of Judah: the window pointing toward Jerusalem, the place where he prayed, the Scripture. At any rate his faith was such a part of him that he would rather die than change the way he prayed. When the king learned Daniel had violated the decree he was angry at himself (Daniel 6:14). He began searching for a way to save Daniel, but he could not (Daniel 6:15). As you read the passage, it appears that the king is more frightened for Daniel than Daniel may have been (Daniel 6:16-18). As morning dawns, he runs to the lion's den and yells, not "Belteshazzar," but "Daniel has your God whom you serve continually, been able to deliver you?" Daniel, whose name means God is judge responds, "My God sent his angel…, because I was found blameless before him."

Thus an exile from Judah influences yet another king in the midst of a corrupt culture toward the God, Jehovah. Wow, what a story! But this is not just a story about Daniel, or Hananiah, Mishael, and Azariah, or their parents. This is a story about how God works in the lives of people just like you, and how he uses them to prepare youth to not just survive in a corrupt culture but thrive. Let's get busy developing the Daniel's God has entrusted to us to influence another corrupt culture toward Him.

notes

1. S. Marikar, Abc News, 5/19/11 http://abcnews.go.com/Entertainment/brad-pitt-katy-perry-back-christian-beliefs/story?id=13620940.
2. Pew Research Center (2010). *Religion Among Milennials*: http://www.pewforum.org/2010/02/17/religion-among-the-millennials.
3. E. J. Young (1977). *The Prophecy of Daniel*. Grand Rapids, MI: Erdmans Publishing.
4. D. Ariely (2012). *The (Honest) Truth About Dishonesty*. New York, NY: Harper Collins.
5. J. G. Baldwin (1978). *Daniel: Tyndale Old Testament Commentaries*. Downers Grove, IL: Intervarsity Press.
6. E. J. Young (1977). *Ibid*.
7. R. Cialdini (1984). *Influence: The Psychology of Persuasion*. New York: Harper Collins.
8. J. J. Arnett, (2000). Emerging adulthood: A theory of development from the late teens through the twenties. *American Psychologist, 55*(5), 469–480. doi:10.1037/0003-066X.55.5.469.
   R. D. Stinson (2010). Hooking up in young adulthood: A review of factors influencing the sexual behavior of college students. *Journal of College Student Psychotherapy, 24*(2), 98–115. doi:10.1080/87568220903558596.
9. C. M. Grello, D. P. Welsh, M. S.., Harper, & J. W. Dickson (2003). Dating and sexual relationship trajectories and adolescent functioning. *Adolescent & Family Health, 3*(3), 103–112.
10. M. L. Fisher, K. Worth, J. R. Garcia, & T. Meredith (2012). Feelings of regret following uncommitted sexual encounters in Canadian university students. *Culture, Health & Sexuality, 14*(1), 45–57. doi:10.1080/13691058.2011.619579.
    W. F. Flack Jr., K. A. Daubman, M. L. Caron, J. A. Asadorian, N. R. D'Aureli, S. N. Gigliotti,...E. R. Stine (2007). Risk factors and consequences of unwanted sex among university students: Hooking up, alcohol, and stress response. *Journal of Interpersonal Violence, 22*(2), 139–157. doi:10.1177/0886260506295354
11. A. Miller (2013). New insights on college drinking: Psychologists' research is pinpointing who is most at risk for drinking problems in college and developing more targeted, evidence-based interventions. *Monitor on Psychology, 44*(9) 46-51.
12. L. D. Johnston, P. M. O'Malley, & J. G. Bachman (2003). *Monitoring the Future National Survey Results on Drug Use, 1975–2002: Vol. II. College Students and Young*

Adults Ages 19–40. (NIH Pub. No. 03–5376). Bethesda, MD: National Institute of Drug Abuse.

13 M. Windle. Alcohol use among adolescents and young adults. National Institute of Alcohol Abuse and Alcoholism. Accessed at http://pubs.niaaa.nih.gov/publications/arh27-1/79-86.htm on December 23, 2013.

14 D. T. Neal, W. Wood, & A. Drolet (2013). How do people adhere to goals when willpower is low? The profits (and pitfalls) of strong habits. *Journal of Personality and Social Psychology, 104*(6), 959-975. doi: 10.1037/a0032626.

15 C. Colson (8/6/2001). Reversing Biblical Memory Loss: The language of faith doesn't have to become a foreign tongue. *Christianity Today:* http://www.christianitytoday.com/ct/2001/august6/31.88.html?paging=off.

16 T. Longman (1999). *Daniel: The NIV Application Commentary.* Grand Rapids, MI: Zondervan Publishing.

17 K. Weir (2013). Never a dull moment. *Monitor on Psychology, 44*(7) 54-57.

18 G. Martin, P. Graham, & C. Burnette (2000). Maximizing Multiple Intelligences Through Multimedia: A Real Application of Gardner's Theories. *Multimedia Schools,* 7 (5).

19 M. Gladwell (2008). *Outliers: The Story of Success.* New York, NY: Little, Brown & Company.

20 L. Hao, & H. S. Woo (2012). Distinct Trajectories in the Transition to Adulthood: Are Children of Immigrants Advantaged? *Child Development, 83*(5), 1623-39, DOI: 10.1111/j.1467-8624.2012.01798.x.

21 L. Winerman (December, 2013). Questionnaire: What sets high achievers apart? Interview with Angela Lee Duckworth. *Monitor on Psychology, 44*(11), 28-31.

22 P. Dolan & L. Kudrna (2013). More Years, Less Yawns: Fresh Evidence on Tiredness by Age and Other Factors. *Journals of Gerontology B Psychological Sciences Social Sciences* first published online November 22, 2013 doi:10.1093/geronb/gbt118.

23 M. Gladwell (2008). *Ibid.*

24 R. Murray (November 21, 2012). Woman on unpaid leave after taking disrespectful photo next to soldier's grave during work trip. *New York Daily News.* http://www.nydailynews.com/news/national/vulgar-facebook-pic-woman-canned-article-1.1205609#ixzz2nE7eQjlw. Accessed November 12, 2013.

25 C. Pearson, L. M. Andersson & C. L. Porath (2005). Workplace Incivility. In *Counterproductive Work Behavior* (Ed. S. Fox & P. E. Spector) pages 177-200. Washington, DC: American Psychological Association.

26 M. Gladwell (2005). *Blink: The Power of Thinking without Thinking.* New York, NY: Little, Brown & Company.

27 D. Goleman (1994). *Emotional Intelligence.* New York, NY: Bantam Books.

28 K. Weir (March, 2012). Revising Your Story: Social Psychologist Timothy D. Wilson argues that behavior change may be easier than we think. *Monitor on Psychology, 43*(3), 28.

29 M. Csikszentmihaly (1997). *Creativity.* New York, NY: Harper Collins.

30 M. Csikszentmihaly (1990). *Flow.* New York, NY: Harper Collins.

31 L. G. Knapp, J. E. Kelly-Reid, & S. A. Ginder (2012). *Enrollment in Postsecondary Institutions, Fall 2011; Financial Statistics, Fiscal Year 2011; and Graduation Rates, Selected Cohorts, 2003-2008.* Washington, DC: U.S. Department of Education. http://nces.ed.gov/pubs2012/2012174rev.pdf)

32 Strong Interest Resource Strategies for Group and Individual Interpretation in College Settings (1995).

33 Strong (1995). Ibid.

34 Strong (1995). Ibid.

35 Strong (1995). Ibid.

36 Strong (1995). Ibid.

37 Strong (1995). Ibid.

38 I. B. Myers, & P. B. Myers (1980). Gifts Differing: Understanding Personality Type. Palo Alto, CA: Davies-Black Publishing, Inc.

39 D. Hembrick (2012). *Eagle Career Network*. Durham, NC: North Carolina Central University.

40 The Federal Trade Commission. *Choosing a Vocational School*. Accessed at http://www.consumer.ftc.gov/articles/0241-choosing-vocational-school on December 26, 2013.

41 N. J. Roese & A. Summerville (2005). What we regret most...and why. *Personality and Social Psychology Bulletin, 31,* 1273-1285. Doi:10.1177/0146167205274693.

42 L. G. Knapp, et al. (2012). *Ibid.*

43 D. J. Foss (2013). *Your complete guide to college success: How to study smart, achieve your goals, and enjoy campus life*. Washington, DC: American Psychological Association.

44 F. Autin & J. C. Croizet (2012). Improving working memory efficiency by reframing metacognitive interpretation of task difficulty. *Journal of Experimental Psychology: General, 141*(4), 610-618.

45 D. J. Foss (2013). *Ibid.*

46 D. J. Foss (2013). *Ibid.*

47 D. J. Foss (2013). *Ibid.*

48 D. J. Foss (2013). *Ibid.*

49 J. L. Walsh, R. Fielder, K. B. Carey & M. P. Carey (March 26, 2013). Female College Students' Media Use and Academic Outcomes: Results from a Longitudinal Cohort. *Emerging Adulthood*, from http://eax.sagepub.com/content/early/2013/03/05/2167696813479780.

50 D. J. Foss (2013). *Ibid.*

51 D. J. Foss (2013). *Ibid.*

52 D. Hembrick (2012). *Ibid.*

53 Gallup. *State of the American Workplace Report 2013: Employee Engagement Insights for U.S. Business Leaders*. Assessed at http://www.gallup.com/strategicconsulting/163007/state-american-workplace.aspx on December 30, 2013. Washington, D.C.:Gallup.

54 D. J. Foss (2013). *Ibid.*

55 M. McPherson, L. Smith-Loving & M. E. Brashers (2006). Social isolation in America: Changes in core discussion networks over two decades. *American Sociological Review, 71,* 353-375.

56 D. Blansky, C. Kavanaugh, C. Boothroyd, B. Benson, J. Gallagher, J. Endress & H. Sayama (2013). Spread of Academic Success in a High School Social Network. *PLoS ONE, 8*(2): e55944 DOI: 10.1371/journal.pone.0055944.

57   S. Burd-Sharps & K. Lewis (2012). *One in Seven*. Brooklyn, New York, NY: Measure of America. Accessed at http://www.measureofamerica.org/wp-content/uploads/2012/09/MOA-One_in_Seven09-14.pdf on December 30, 2013.

58   M. Gladwell (2005). *Ibid.*

59   A. Miller (October, 2013). The science of karma: Organizational psychology and top-rated Wharton professor Adam Grant says one secret to success is helping other succeed. *Monitor on Psychology, 44*(9), 28.

60   M. McPherson, L. Smith-Loving & M. E. Brashers (2006). Social isolation in America: Changes in core discussion networks over two decades. *American Sociological Review, 71,* 353-375.

61   M. E. Brashears (2011). "Small networks and high isolation?: A reexamination of American discussion networks." *Social Networks. 33*(4): 331-341.

62   A. K. Przybylski, & N. Weinstein (2013). Can you connect with me now? How the presence of mobile communication technology influences face-to-face conversation quality. *Journal of Social and Personal Relationships, 30* (3), 237-246.

63   D. Cohn, J. S. Passel, W. Wang & G. Livingston (December 14, 2011). Barely Half of U.S. Adults Are Married—A Record Low. *Pew Research Social Demographics and Change.* Washington, D.C.: Pew Research Center. Assessed at http://www.pewsocialtrends.org/2011/12/14/barely-half-of-u-s-adults-are-married-a-record-low/ on December 31, 2013.

64   J. Gottman (1995). *Why Marriages Succeed or Fail.* New York, NY: Fireside. Lessons From the "Marriage Lab." By: Monaghan, Peter, Chronicle of Higher Education, 00095982, 2/26/99, Vol. 45, Issue 25.

65   D. J. Simpson (1977). *The Book of Daniel.* Nashville, TN: Randall House Publications.

66   S. L. Vasiliauskas & M. R. McMinn (2012). The Effects of a Prayer Intervention on the Process of Forgiveness. *Psychology of Religion and Spirituality, 5*(1), 23-32.

67   R. D. Enright (2001). *Forgiveness is a Choice.* Washington, DC: American Psychological Association.

68   A. Sagi-Schwartz, M. J. Bakermans-Kranenburg, S. Linn & M. H. van IJzendoorn (2013). *Against All Odds: Genocidal Trauma Is Associated with Longer Life-Expectancy of the Survivors.* PLoS ONE 8(7): e69179. doi:10.1371/journal.pone.0069179.

69   C. Tara Marshall (2012). *Cyberpsychology, Behavior, and Social Networking, 15* (10): 521-526. doi:10.1089/cyber.2012.0125.

DON'T LET FEAR HOLD YOU BACK.

MOVE BEYOND THE PAIN AND STEP OUT INTO FREEDOM.

The author shares details concerning the **emotional and physical symptoms** related to the subject as well as ways to overcome these difficulties.

Readers will find **words of comfort and hope** through Scripture, examples from the Bible of those dealing with difficulties, and practical advice on surviving the difficult situation they are facing.

A **list of resources** is given to encourage further help where needed.

randall house
randallhouse.com
(800) 877-7030

d6family.com

SURVIVING CULTURE
When Character and Your World Collide

13-ISBN: 9780892656875 Price: $9.99

You are faced with many challenges that attempt to lure you away from the truth of Scripture and your foundation of faith. Dr. Moody shares strong advice on the need to be prepared and make wise decisions to navigate the culture of today. He supports his points with relevant facts and current statistics. He also shows how the culture Daniel faced in Old Testament times correlates with some of the same trials teens face today. Daniel and his companions faced unbelievable pressure to compromise their faith living in a corrupt culture. They not only survived but thrived and had a real impact on the world around them. Dr. Moody shares how young people today can do the same.

randall house
randallhouse.com
1-800-877-7030

A must for parenting in a digital worl

- Be informed about safety and awareness in online browsing
- Discover truths about Internet pornography an its draw for teens
- Talk with your child about texting and sexting
- Set time limits and restrictions with video gam
- Understand the role of social networking in the lives of teens
- Learn to protect your high schooler's online reputation
- And many more issues

TECH SAVVY PARENTIN
BY BRIAN HOUSMAN

randall hous
randallhouse.com
1-800-877-7030